CREATING GEORGIA

CREATING

GEORGIA

MINUTES OF
THE BRAY ASSOCIATES
1730–1732
&
SUPPLEMENTARY
DOCUMENTS

EDITED BY RODNEY M. BAINE

The University of Georgia Press
Athens & London

Paperback edition, 2010
© 1995 by the University of Georgia Press
Athens, Georgia 30602
www.ugapress.org
All rights reserved
Designed by Walton Harris
Set in 10/14 Janson by Tseng Information Systems, Inc.
Printed digitally in the United States of America

The Library of Congress has cataloged the hardcover edition
of this book as follows:
Library of Congress Cataloging-in-Publication Data
LCCN Permalink: http://lccn.loc.gov/94004169

Creating Georgia : minutes of the Bray Associates, 1730–1732
& supplementary documents / edited by Rodney M. Baine.
xxvi, 162 p. ; 23 cm.
ISBN 0-8203-1666-0 (alk. paper)
Includes bibliographical references (p. 127–145) and index.
1. Georgia—Politics and government—To 1775—Sources. I.
Baine, Rodney M. II. Bray Associates.
F289 .C74   1995
975.8'01 20   94-4169

Paperback ISBN-13: 978-0-8203-3524-7
ISBN-10: 0-8203-3524-X

British Library Cataloging-in-Publication Data available

On the title page: An engraving by an unknown artist, based
on the William Hogarth painting of James Oglethorpe's prison
committee examining Jacob Mendez Solas in Fleet Prison.
From the members of this committee, Oglethorpe recruited
most of the Bray Associates and the Georgia Trustees.
(Hargrett Rare Book and Manuscript Library, University of
Georgia Libraries)

For Edith, Farrell, and Meg

CONTENTS

Preface
ix

Introduction
xiii

Bray Minutes, 1730–1732,
and Supplementary Documents
1

Postscript
117

Appendix
119

Notes
127

Index
147

PREFACE

In 1732, as students of Georgia history know, the Georgia Trustees were named from the revived and reorganized Bray Associates. But from 1730 to 1732, before these associates became the Georgia Trustees and while they were planning the colony and securing the Georgia Charter, they kept minutes of their deliberations. Now deposited at the Rhodes House Library in Oxford, these minutes were microfilmed in 1929 for distribution by the Library of Congress. Unfortunately, few Georgia historians seem to be using them. No wonder. The tops and bottoms of some frames have become so blackened by time that many sentences there are illegible, and in many frames the right-hand margins are so blurred that words or parts of words are obliterated. Moreover, the associates devoted much of their time to providing parochial libraries and assisting in Christianizing the slaves in America. It has seemed best, however, to reproduce these early minutes in their entirety—up until the time when the Georgia Trustees began to meet separately from the parent group and assumed sole responsibility for the new colony. The minutes are, after all, the most important historical source for our understanding of the Georgia genesis.

Unfortunately, these minutes reveal little about obtaining the Georgia Charter. The associates delegated to a committee, named by Oglethorpe, the securing of that charter; but this committee rarely reported to the associates, and the minutes record few details. Primarily to record the progress of that committee, I have interspersed entries from the the sources that do: the *Diary of Viscount Percival, Afterwards First Earl of Egmont*; Percival's unpublished "Account of Georgia: The Leading Steps to His Maj[est]y's Grant of the Charter," from the British Library; the Journals of the Commissioners for Trade and Plantations; and the Journals of the Committee of the Privy Council for America and the West Indies, both of these last from the Public Record Office. I have also included Dr. Thomas Bray's feoffment of the Bray Associates, on January 15, 1730.

The printed records—John Percival's *Diary* and three documents from *Acts of the Privy Council of England, Colonial Series*—I have reproduced as they appear in the original except that I have replaced with curved braces the rectangular brackets there. Spaced periods, or suspension points in the *Diary* or in Dr. Bray's feoffment indicate my omissions. In the manuscripts, including the minutes, I have retained the spelling, capitalization, and punctuation of the original. I have, however, lowered the superior letters of abbreviations and have replaced with the letters *th* the thorn (*þ*), which in the eighteenth century appears as *y*. Thus *ye* and *yt* appear here as *the* and *that*. I have also changed to follow our present usage the quotation marks that in the eighteenth century begin every quoted line; and I have indented the Reverend Mr. Smith's early paragraphs, which he failed to indent from May 27 until November 11, 1732.

Since we are not especially interested here in secretarial style, I have usually ignored the canceled passages that the secretary patently corrected or improved in the process of recording his minutes. In the minutes I have, however, enclosed in angle brackets the rejected readings of words and passages in the minutes that were probably revised or corrected at the secretary's own initiative or at the suggestion of the chairman at the end of the meeting, or sometimes even canceled by vote of those present when the minutes were read at the following meeting. In the other manuscripts I have followed a similar practice. In reproducing these manuscripts I have preferred the original, rough copy to a subsequent fair copy, and these to later transcripts. In the minutes I have ignored or

PREFACE

mentioned only in a note the annotations made later by a different hand; and I have relegated to notes, with slashes to indicate new lines, the subject headings that appear sporadically in the left margin. Square brackets enclose my editorial intrusions, except in Percival's "Account," where they are by Phinizy Spalding, of the history department at the University of Georgia. Three spaced hyphens indicate spaces deliberately left blank in the manuscript to allow subsequent insertions.

Without a fresh microfilm made for me at the Bodleian Library through the kind cooperation of Rhodes House Library, Oxford, where the original is now deposited, I would for many readings have had to rely on guesswork. For the few readings that even then remained difficult, I am greatly indebted to Alan S. Bell, Esq., librarian at Rhodes House Library, who, assisted by archivist Clare Brown, checked the most difficult passages against the original. The new microfilm is now in the Hargrett Rare Book and Manuscript Library at the University of Georgia. For a typescript of Percival's "Account of Georgia," I am indebted to my colleague Phinizy Spalding, who generously read and critiqued early versions of my introduction and appendix.

For permission to publish these minutes and the Bray feoffment, I am grateful to the United Society for the Propagation of the Gospel; and for the feoffment, I also thank the University of Illinois Press for its assistance. For permission to quote Percival's separate account, I am indebted to the Trustees of the British Library.

INTRODUCTION

Although the genesis of the Georgia colony has received considerable attention, particularly in accounts by Albert B. Saye and Verner W. Crane,[1] their divergent views have left considerable confusion concerning the father of the colony and the constituency of its founders. Saye emphasized the role of the merchants in its origin and suggested that Georgia may have been the brainchild of Captain Thomas Coram. Crane stressed the contributions of the clergymen and credited the concept to the Reverend Thomas Bray. (For an examination of their arguments, please see the Appendix.)

But as these Bray minutes and ancillary documents clearly show, Colonial Georgia owed its creation and its shaping to the vision, energy, and determination of James Edward Oglethorpe. And his most numerous and effective colleagues in its shaping were neither clergymen nor merchants, but the members of Parliament whom he recruited from his prison committees. It is all the more important, then, to make availaible the documents that tell the story of that creation.

Clearly Oglethorpe was influenced by such writers and colonizers as Sir Josiah Child, William Penn, Jean Pierre Purry, and perhaps Joshua Gee. But Georgia was Oglethorpe's dream. Of course he had among the Bray Associates the able assistance of many colleagues, like Viscount Percival, James Vernon, Captain Thomas Coram, several dedicated clergymen, and the members of Parliament whom he drew from his prison committees. And when he needed additional help he called on others who were not associates.

Early in 1729, long before he met Dr. Bray, Oglethorpe took the first step toward creating the Georgia colony, for on February 13, 1730, he informed Percival that he had been able "in one year's time" to secure funds toward that purpose.[2] Almost as soon as he began his work on reform in the London debtor prisons, he must have realized that some provision must be made for the released debtors so that they would not perforce return to a new incarceration. He decided on a charitable colony as their best opportunity. Since at that time most Englishmen believed that almost any emigrant was a loss to the mother country, he felt that instead of battling opposition in Parliament, he would seek funding through private charity, beginning with whatever benevolent funds were available. As he became involved in litigation toward that end, he became convinced that he could achieve his objective only if he worked through some legally recognized benevolent group. As he told Percival, two of the three trustees of the Joseph King bequest had consented to a decree in his favor "on condition that the trust should be annexed to some trusteeship already in being."[3] The best-known and most-effective charitable organizations were those created by the Reverend Thomas Bray (1658–1730).

Dr. Bray was a devout cleric, rector of Sheldon since 1690 and rector also of St. Botolph's, Aldgate, in London, from 1706. He was an able scholar and writer on church doctrine and was especially respected for his *Catechetical Lectures* (1696). He is best remembered, however, for his work as an administrator. In 1700 he visited Maryland in his capacity of religious commissary, a position he held from 1695 until 1703. He founded the Society for the Promotion of Christian Knowledge (SPCK) in 1699 and secured its charter in 1701, along with that of the Society for the Propagation of the Gospel in Foreign Parts (SPG), which he also founded. These very large and effective organizations, however, were unlikely to be diverted from their original purposes to support a colonizing project; and they would certainly have expected complete control thereof.

A more likely group was the Bray Associates, whose religious work has been thoroughly documented by John C. Van Horne's 1979 dissertation, " 'Pious Designs,' " and his *Religious Philanthropy and Colonial Slavery: The American Correspondence of the Associates of Dr. Bray, 1717–1777*.[4] This small group originated even earlier, in 1699, with a donation made to Dr. Bray by King William's secretary, Abel Tassein, Sieur D'Allone, toward Christianizing the blacks in America. Only after D'Allone died, however, in 1723, did his will provide adequate funds so that Dr. Bray could set up a permanent charitable group to administer them. On January 15, 1724, Dr. Bray named four associates to work with him toward Christianizing slaves in the colonies and supplying parochial libraries: Robert Hales, clerk of the King's Privy Council; his brother the Reverend Stephen Hales, botanist, physiologist, and inventor, with ties to the royal family; William Belitha, of Kingston upon Thames; and John Viscount Percival, a member of Oglethorpe's prison committee. They seem to have met at Dr. Bray's discretion, irregularly; and if they kept minutes, these have apparently not survived. Gradually the associates became virtually inactive, especially after 1727, when Bray became quite ill, and certainly in 1729, when he became bedridden.

In December of 1729 Oglethorpe visited the infirm humanitarian and asked him to expand his associates so that they could acquire and administer part of the King legacy for his proposed colony. Dr. Bray gave his assistance without stint, and he even invested Oglethorpe with the guidance of the revived Bray Associates and deferred to him in the selection of the new associates. Twenty-eight new members were to be added to the original five (minus Robert Hales, who was apparently implicated and imprisoned in connection with his brother William's forgery—writing a bad check for sixty-four hundred pounds).[5] On January 15, 1730, Dr. Bray signed the necessary feoffment naming the new trustees.

He died a month later, and eight others did not record their acceptance of trusteeship and failed to attend any meeting, at least until after the Georgia Charter was secured.[6]

Of the twenty new members who accepted the trust and took part in the creation of the Georgia colony, only four were clergymen. The learned Reverend John Burton, a friend and contemporary of Oglethorpe at Christ Church, Oxford, and in 1730 a tutor there, attended only rarely. The other three were quite active: the brilliant oriental scholar and mathematician Arthur Bedford, who served as the first recording secretary; the Reverend Richard Bundy, chaplain in ordinary to the king (surely suggested by Oglethorpe, for Dr. Bray apparently did not know him); and the Reverend Samuel Smith, Dr. Bray's assistant and a secretary for the associates. To these was soon added the Reverend Daniel Somerscales, Somerscale, or Somerscald, vicar of Doddington, in Kent.

Three were neither priests nor politicians. Adam Anderson, a clerk at the South Sea House, destined to become "the historian of commerce," was evidently Oglethorpe's choice. Captain Thomas Coram, a parishioner of Dr. Bray, was quite familiar with colonial America and had been trying for years to create his colony of Georgeia in Nova Scotia. Even more important to the group was James Vernon, clerk of the Privy Council, a body whose approval of the new colony was necessary. Vernon had not been a member of Parliament since 1708-10, but his brother Admiral Edward Vernon was serving on Oglethorpe's prison committee.

The rest of the new associates, thirteen in all including Oglethorpe, were members of Parliament; and with the exception of Colonel George Carpenter, who was not an M.P. during the period 1727-41, and Edward Digby, were all members of Oglethorpe's jails committees, all trustworthy colleagues who had proved to be concerned about human suffering. As Percival remarked in his "Account of Georgia," "The frequent meeting of the Gentlemen concerned, gave us an opportunity to discern who among us had most the public good at hea[rt], or had leasure to attend such services as required pains and application, and were likely without interested views to pursue them. Hence arose a familiarity between many of our Committee, which disposed them to joyn together in any new work that carry'd the face of public util[ity]."⁷

Those whom Oglethorpe selected from his prison committees were Edward Harley, one of the king's auditors; Rogers Holland, who was involved in the prosecutions of both wardens Bambridge and Huggins; Robert Hucks; Edward Hughes, judge advocate of the army, who had headed Oglethorpe's committee during its examination of Lord Chief Justice Robert Eyre; John Laroche, of Huguenot extraction; the wealthy Sir James Lowther, F.R.S.; Robert More; John Viscount Percival, later Lord Egmont, an original associate; Major Charles Selwyn, equerry to the queen; William Sloper; and Thomas Tower. To these thirteen must be added two more members of the prison committee who were not named in Dr. Bray's new feoffment but who became active in the Bray Associates by July of 1730: Francis Eyles and George Heathcote, nephew of the influential Sir Gilbert Heathcote, governor of the Bank of England. An alderman of London elected Lord Mayor in 1740, George Heathcote was to serve the Georgia Trustees as its treasurer. Fifteen, all told, the members of Parliament easily outnumbered the clerics and other associates; and it is on this group that Oglethorpe relied to secure the Georgia Charter and, ultimately, to secure the necessary parliamentary subventions. To them, the others also left the selection of the colonists.

Before Dr. Bray signed his new feoffment, Oglethorpe evidently approached some of the prospective members to elicit their cooperation. But since Parliament was not sitting, many members were not then in London; and when the new session began, Oglethorpe felt more pressed to reactivate his prison committee. Not until Friday, February 13, 1730, did he approach Percival concerning his charitable colony. As Percival recorded in his *Diary*, "being informed that I was a trustee for Mr. Dalone's legacy, who left about a thousand pounds to convert negroes, he had proposed me and my associates as proper persons to be made trustees of this new affair; that the old gentlemen [the King trustees] approved of us, and he hoped I would accept it in conjunction with himself, and several of our Committee of Gaols." His plan, Oglethorpe explained, was "to procure a quantity of acres either from the Government or by gift or purchase in the West Indies,[8] and to plant thereon a hundred miserable wretches who being let out of gaol by the last year's Act,[9] are now starving about the town for want of employment; that they should be settled all together by way of colony."[10]

At their first meeting, on March 21, 1730, the newly reconstituted Bray Associates realized that they faced a considerable obstacle in securing legal recognition. Percival, who had returned to his home at Charlton only on January 8, 1730, had not signed the new feoffment; several of the Christian names of the new associates had been omitted; and Dr. Bray had died before these deficiencies could be supplied. Percival's attorney, Francis Annesley, a member of Oglethorpe's prison committee, held that their difficulties could be settled only before the Master of the Rolls.[11] Consequently at their second meeting, on May 12, the associates asked Oglethorpe to seek legal recognition. At the following meeting, on July 1, he reported to the group that on June 24 he had placed the difficulty before Sir Joseph Jekyll, Master of the Rolls and a member of his prison committee, who "gave a final decree, the most advantageous to the Society, which could be desired, and appointed the Gentlemen, who were Associates to Dr Bray to act as Trustees for Executing Mr D'Allone's Will."

The new Bray Associates encountered difficulties not only in securing legal recognition: they were unable to acquire any considerable legacy or bequest for their charitable colony: the Joseph King legacy, of which they were led to believe that they had acquired five thousand pounds; the funds that had been allocated to Bishop George Berkeley by Parliament for a college in Bermuda; or the legacy of forty thousand pounds left for charity in

1729 by Thomas Tufton, sixth earl of Thanet. Indeed, the associates became desperate enough to accept Sir Robert Walpole's offer of tickets in the government lottery, in order to resell them at a profit.

In spite of Oglethorpe's confidence and the assurance of the Lord Chancellor, Peter King, first baron King of Ockham, the Georgia Trustees apparently never received any of the expected funds from the Joseph King bequest. In July 1730, as Percival recorded in his "Account of Georgia," "I attended Mr. Oglethorp into the City to pay a visit to Mr. Carpenter, one of the old Trustees lately mentioned, to thank him for his promised bounty to the Associates, when to our great surprise and disappointment, He acquainted us that he had been advised that the disposal of any part of the charity in the way he gave us hopes of, was not suitable to the deceased's will." When Percival returned from his vacation, in June, he learned "that the old man was not to be moved from his purpose of withold[ing] the Associates the 5000 £ expected."[12] It is one of the minor myths of the Georgia genesis, supported by such able scholars as R. A. Roberts and Amos Aschbach Ettinger, that Oglethorpe actually secured five thousand pounds from the King legacy to finance his first settlement.[13]

For a while Oglethorpe and Percival attempted to woo their friend George Berkeley to divert to their new colony some of the money that Parliament had authorized for his Bermuda college. But even if the diversion had been possible, Berkeley himself preferred Yale College to the new colony. Only in 1733, while Oglethorpe was in Georgia, did Parliament assign to the Georgia colony ten thousand pounds from the very St. Christopher money from which they had earlier voted to fund Berkeley's college.

Later the associates turned to the Thanet legacy, which had theoretically been available after the will was first probated, in January of 1730. On February 11, 1731, Adam Anderson reported to the associates that one thousand pounds from this charity was available for a particular charity, and the associates then agreed to turn to that legacy for the new colony. Percival tried diligently but ineffectively, at first, to secure ten thousand pounds, and subsequently the stated maximum of one thousand pounds. This amount they apparently received through Matthew Lambe on October 17, 1733, in addition to a token three hundred pounds late in 1732.[14]

Although it had evidently not been their original purpose to go to Parliament for a subvention, the associates were eventually forced to do so. Not only did they fail to secure adequate funds from any charitable legacy for their colony, but during the first few months their objective became more ambitious. At first they had planned only to settle a hundred families somewhere—a smaller version of Purry's South Carolina colony. But their ambitions widened to envision a separate province, a group of settlements, or "colonies" between South Carolina and Spanish Florida. Consequently they now began to advertise not only their humanitarian purposes but also the military and economic advantages that the mother country would gain through the new colony. At first they decided to request ten thousand pounds in parliamentary funding to take vagrant boys off the streets of London and to bind them as apprentices to masters of crafts and trades among the Georgia colonists.

For a brief time some of the associates thought of binding them as apprentices to inactivated soldiers. This idea, probably the suggestion of Captain Coram, who had planned to use such soldiers for his colony of Georgeia in Nova Scotia, was short-lived. Even though part of the promotional campaign, now perforce directed especially toward Parliament, pointed out the advantages of establishing a colony to the south of South Carolina, Oglethorpe and most of the other associates intended to rely on the militia for the defense of the colony. Only two inactivated soldiers came to Georgia as colonists during the first decade. Evidently it was left up to the members of Parliament to proceed as they thought best with their attempt to secure parliamentary funds; and the next

INTRODUCTION

day Oglethorpe proceeded with the plan, both he and Heathcote speaking for it before the House. It was, however, defeated.

Meanwhile, in order to augment one of the large private windfalls that they still hoped for, the associates began at once to seek for gifts with which to help establish the new charity; and it was on such donations that they had to depend for the first transport, on the *Anne*. On July 15, 1730, Oglethorpe reported a gift of twenty pounds toward that purpose; and three days later Percival recorded that Colonel Schutz had given him ten pounds from the Prince William's charity money for the same charity. They received other sums from time to time, such as the promise of one hundred pounds from stationer Thomas Page on March 11, 1731. On August 30, 1730, at the same meeting at which the associates signed their petition to the king for a grant of lands, they also drew up and signed a paper for the indefatigable Captain Coram "to carry to Tunbridge in order to collect subscriptions to our scheme." On June 8, 1732, when it became clear that the charter would be soon forthcoming, the associates approved the printing of commissions for collecting contributions toward the new colony.

In addition to problems of securing legal recognition and funding, Oglethorpe experienced some difficulties in organizing the associates effectively. In his initial conversation with Percival concerning the charitable colony, he had promised that a new member would commit himself to furthering only the designs of the associates that interested him. Apparently Oglethorpe did not think that the members of his prison committee would be expected to attend meetings devoted to parochial libraries or to the Christianization of plantation slaves—unless they chose to do so. At their meeting of July 30, 1730, with Oglethorpe and Percival both present, the associates agreed that they would subsequently hold separate monthly meetings for each of their three main designs and a fourth meeting "to read over all such Deeds, Wills, and other Papers," and that the secretary should give advanced

xxi

notice of the business of each meeting. Subsequently this resolution was struck out, and the business of every meeting remained general. Finally, however, on October 2, 1730, with Oglethorpe in the chair, a special committee was appointed to deal with all matters of parochial libraries, the most tedious aspect of the associates' work, so that the parliamentary members could be spared these details. For the parliamentary associates, who were often, like Percival, absent from London outside of term time, were men selected by Oglethorpe for their dedication to their duties, and some of them could not spare the time from their parliamentary attendance and committee duties to authorize proper distribution and care of devotional materials. During the early months, however, chairman Oglethorpe was authorized to call a meeting only when there was necessary business to attend to.

Before the associates could effectively advertise for private funds and colonists for the new charitable colony, they had of course to secure a royal charter. They gave Oglethorpe complete control of this important function. Toward this purpose the associates agreed on July 1, 1730, that Oglethorpe and "such other Persons of this Society, whom he shall desire for his Assistance" should endeavor to "obtain a Grant of Lands in America." During that month Oglethorpe, Vernon, Percival, and some of the other members of the prison committee drafted the proper petition.[15] On July 30, "A Petition to the King's most excellent Majesty, desiring a Grant of certain Lands in America for the better Maintainance of the poor of this Kingdom, was read, and signed by the Members then present." It was also agreed "that it be signed by all the other Members as soon as possible, and presented to His Majesty." Subsequently this resolution was deleted from the record, probably because a later minute of the same meeting was more precise: "Mr Vernon laid a Draught of a Petition to the King, for the Grant of certain Lands to the Southward of Carolina" before the associates and it was "Agreed that the Petition be empressed and signed."

On September 17, 1730, the petition of Percival, Oglethorpe, and the nineteen other associates who became the first Georgia Trustees was presented to the King's Privy Council and there referred to a committee, doubtless the Committee on Plantations. On December 3, 1730, it was returned to the Privy Council for action, and here it was not unexpectedly referred to the Board of Trade and Plantations. The membership of the charter committee seems to have been formalized soon afterward, for on January 14, 1731, the associates agreed that the "Committee for Solliciting the Grant" should consist of Percival, Col. Carpenter, Mr. Hucks, Mr. Towers, Mr. Eyles, Mr. La Roche, Oglethorpe, and Mr. More. Probably James Vernon was not included because he could then act more freely as secretary of the Privy Council in helping to steer the charter through its tortuous course. On January 28, 1731, Oglethorpe reported to the associates the progress that he had made and secured an expression of their confidence.

Then for almost a year, delays were numerous and vexatious, as all alterations proposed had to be cleared by the Board of Trade and Plantations as well as by the King's Privy Council; and the attorney general and the solicitor general took months to draft the charter. When everybody else was satisfied, King George II for several additional months refused to sign it.

Although the delays in securing the charter were certainly frustrating, they could not have been entirely unexpected, and Oglethorpe and the other associates knew that they could rely on the assistance of several of their present or former colleagues on the King's Privy Council and the Board of Trade. James Vernon had been a clerk of the Privy Council ever since 1701 and clerk in ordinary, or secretary, since 1715. The Board of Trade included not only the faithful and influential Martin Bladen, but also Edward Ashe and Sir Thomas Franklin, all of them members of Oglethorpe's prison committees. Unfortunately Percival was out of London during much of the year, but Oglethorpe, with a few others aptly chosen, was always available to explain and persuade before the Privy Council or the Board of Trade.

Of the problems that the associates encountered, the most crucial was the appointment of Georgia's civil and military officers, especially those of the militia. This difficulty strained the tempers of the charter committee so much that at times some of them were tempted to give up the whole project. From the beginning, the petition of the associates named, as commander of the Georgia militia, the governor of South Carolina, then Colonel Robert Johnson, with whom they began an early correspondence. Apparently the associates wanted to place in Colonel Johnson's hands some of the responsibility for the safety of the colony; but they were unwilling to grant him the appointment of the officers of their militia.

Obviously, as I have argued elsewhere on other grounds,[16] Oglethorpe did not originally intend to lead the colonists to Georgia. Captain Coram did, and Coram's friends, such as Henry Newman, secretary of the SPCK, spread abroad Coram's intention.[17] But Captain Coram had captained a ship in the merchant marine. Oglethorpe had served in several campaigns against the Saracens under Prince Eugene of Savoy;[18] and when war with the Spaniards broke out, he was, because of this experience, placed in command of the combined forces, regulars as well as militia, of both Georgia and South Carolina. Had Oglethorpe realized in 1730 or 1731 that he would head the initial transport and remain in Georgia, off and on, for almost a decade, he would have demanded and probably been given command of the Georgia militia under the Georgia Charter.

The minutes of the associates also reveal the beginnings that they made toward cultivating friendly relationships with the bishop of London, who was in charge of the Anglican Church in the colonies, and the two associations that would assist them considerably in their enterprise—the SPCK and the SPG. At their third meeting they resolved to approach these two organizations through members who belonged to each group, to cultivate a good mutual understanding; and to request the cooperation of the bishop of London, who headed the colonial clergy, they appointed a committee consisting of Oglethorpe, Vernon, Bedford, and Bundy. They quickly established a warm and fruitful cooperation. The SPCK was to finance the transportation of the Salzburghers to Georgia; and the SPG, the expenses of the clergymen there.

Provision for their promotional literature, the associates arranged early. On November 12, 1730, they agreed that Oglethorpe should write a treatise "to encourage all charitable Persons to contribute towards the charitable Colony," and on February 4, 1732, when the charter seemed finally to be in the offing, several of the associates, including Oglethorpe, Percival, and doubtless Captain Coram, "prepared a draft of an account of our design in order to be printed."[19] Only in 1990 did Oglethorpe's tract, *Some Account of the Design of the Trustees for establishing Colonys in America*, finally appear. But it provided material for Benjamin Martyn's *Some Account of the Designs of the Trustees* (1732); and a week before Martyn's brief tract appeared, Oglethorpe published, in the *London Journal*, an anonymous appeal for benefactions.[20]

Long before the Bray Associates became the Georgia Trustees, they interviewed applicants who wished to immigrate to the new colony and even considered applicants for the first ministry there. On March 11, 1731, Michael Terry, of Ludgate Hill, and Sebastian Trottman, of St. Martins le Grand, applied to go to Georgia; but since the M.P.'s were then absent, both were told to attend at the next meeting. On March 25, Stephen Lee, of Lemon St., Goodman's Fields, applied to go with his wife, daughter, and three sons. On April 8, the associates read a letter from another prospective emigrant, a Mr. John Copping, apothecary, chirurgeon, and schoolmaster, offering himself and a neighbor, a shoemaker; and at the same meeting, John Adderly, a weaver of St. Leonard's, Shoreditch, volunteered himself, his wife, two sons, and a daughter. When Mr. Joseph Bonner applied as a minister for Georgia, the associates requested of him only a certificate from the University of Edinburgh, but they obviously preferred a Cambridge or Oxford graduate.

Thus in the creation of the colony, the minutes of the associates and ancillary documents show clearly that Oglethorpe was both creator and architect. He was elected the first chairman of the Bray Associates. Their very first resolution was to give him complete control. The associates "were willing to do whatever shall be thought proper for them to promote so good a Design, and Mr Oglethorpe was desired to take such Measures, as he should think proper for Making the same successful." He was given authority to name his own charter committee. For a while he was even empowered to set the meetings—to summon the associates when he thought that they had adequate business to consider. Of course he could not attend every meeting, once a fairly regular schedule had been established. He was still chairman of the important parliamentary committee on prisons; and even when that committee had finished its work, other parliamentary duties sometimes demanded his attention. But he was everywhere in control, as the minutes and supplementary documents show. Without his determination, his vision of a charitable colony would have been only a sentimental dream. Moreover, he had the determination and skill to make his dream into a reality. He was the architect of Georgia, seeing the charter through the Board of Trade and the King's Privy Council. He then became chief builder and defender, twice returning to England in order to persuade the ministry to protect the colony from Spanish claims and in order to secure from Parliament the funds needed for the desperate settlers. He devoted his considerable fortune and risked his life to protect his colony. Without Oglethorpe, the region might have become temporarily part of Spanish Florida, by forfeit or by conquest. Never before or after did an American colony owe so much to one man.

BRAY MINUTES, 1730-1732
AND SUPPLEMENTARY DOCUMENTS

[*John, Viscount Percival, February 13, 1730*]

I met Mr. Oglethorp, who informed me that he had found out a very considerable charity, even fifteen thousand pounds, which lay in trustees' hands, and was like to have been lost, because the heir of the testator being one of the trustees, refused to concur with the other two, in any methods for disposing the money, in hopes, as they were seventy years old each of them, they would die soon, and he should remain only surviving trustee, and then might apply it all to his own use. That the two old men were very honest and desirous to be discharged of their burthen, and had concurred with him to get the money lodged in a Master of Chancery's hands till new trustees should be appointed to dispose thereof in a way that should be approved of by them in conjunction with the Lord Chancellor.[1] That the heir of the testator had opposed this, and there had been a lawsuit thereupon, which Oglethorp had carried against the heir, who appealed against the decree; but my Lord Chancellor had confirmed it, and it was a pleasure to him to have been able in one year's time to be able at law to settle this affair. That the trustees had consented to this on condition that the trust should be annexed to some trusteeship already in being, and that being informed that I was a trustee for Mr. Dalone's legacy, who left about a thousand pounds to convert negroes, he had proposed me and my associates as proper persons to be made trustees of this new affair; that the old gentlemen approved of us, and he hoped I would accept it in conjunction with himself, and several of our Committee of Gaols, as Mr. Towers, Mr. Hughes, Mr. Holland, Major Selwyn, and some other gentlemen of worth, as Mr. Sloper and Mr. Vernon, Commissioner of the Excise. I told him it was a pleasure to me to hear his great industry in recovering and securing so great a charity, and to be joined with gentlemen whose worth I knew so well; that I had indeed been thinking to quit the trusteeship of Dalone's legacy, because we were but four, and two of them were rendered incapable of serving and the third was a person I never saw. That when I accepted the Trusteeship it was in order to assist Dean Berkley's Bermuda scheme, by erecting a Fellowship in his college for instructing negroes; that in so doing the charity would be rendered perpetual, whereas to dribble it away in sums of five or ten pounds to missioners in the plantations, the money would be lost without any effect. He answered, experience had shown that religion would not be propagated in the Indies by colleges, besides the Dean had quitted the thoughts of Bermuda, to settle at Rhode Island, and the Government would never give him the twenty thousand pounds promised. I answered the Dean would go to Bermuda, or anywhere the Government should like better, if they would pay him the money. He said, the best way for instructing the negroes would be by finding out conscientious clergymen in the plantations, who would do their endeavours that way without any reward, and that the money might go in sending over religious books for the negroes' use.

He then returned to the new trusteeship, and said that though annexed to this of Dalone's, Dalone's legacy might be a matter remaining distinct from the scheme he proposed for employing the charity he had acquainted me with, and that he designed the new trusteeship should be so drawn that no trustee should be answerable for the actions of the rest, but only for what he signed to. That he had acquainted the Speaker,[2] and some other considerable persons, with his scheme, who approved it much, and there remained only my Lord Chancellor's opinion to be known. That he must tell me by the way, the old trustees of the fifteen thousand pounds would as yet allow but five thousand pounds to be under our management, which sum would answer the scheme; that the scheme is to procure a quantity of acres either from the Government or by gift or purchase in the West Indies, and to plant thereon a hundred miserable wretches who being let out of gaol by the last year's Act, are now starving about the town for want of employment; that they should be settled all together by way of colony, and be subject to subordinate rulers, who should inspect their behaviour and labour under one chief head; that in time they with their families would increase so fast as to become a security and defence of our possessions against the French and Indians of those parts; that they should be employed in cultivating flax and hemp, which being allowed to make into yarn, would be returned to England and Ireland, and greatly promote our manufactures. All which I approved.[3]

[*Dr. Bray's Feoffment, January 15, 1730*]

To all People to who these Presents shall come The Reverend Thomas Bray of St. Buttolph's without Aldgate Doctor of Divinity and his Associates (Vizt:) The Right honourable the Lord Viscount Percival of the Kingdom of Ireland Robert Hales Esqr. late Clerk of his Majesty's most Honourable Privy Councel the Reverend Stephen Hales of Teddington in the County of Middlesex Clerk and William Belitha of London send Greeting *Whereas* Mr. Abel Tassin d'Allone late of the Hague in Holland deceased in and by his last Will and Testament in Writing bearing Date the first day of July (new Stile) which was in the year of our Lord One thousand seven hundred twenty and one Did (amongst other things) will declare order and direct that the fifth part or portion of his English Estate should be divided into two equal parts one part thereof to be delivered to the said Reverend Doctor Thomas Bray and his Associates That a Capital Fund or Stock might be made thereof and that the yearly Income or Produce thereof should be bestowed and imployed in the Erecting a School or Schools for the thorough instructing in the Christian Religion the young Children of the Negroe Slaves and such of their Parents as should show themselves inclinable and desirous of such Instruction in some one or other part of the English Plantations in the West Indies according to such Scheme as should be made. And did thereby further bequeath unto the said Doctor Thomas Bray and his Associates to and for the same Purposes therein and herein before expressed all the Arrears of his Pension from his late Majesty that should be owing to him at the time of his Decease.... *And Whereas* the said Doctor Thomas Bray and his said Associates find themselves under great Difficulties in pursuing the said Design by reason of the Smallness of their Number *And Whereas* the said Robert Hales on account of diverse Affairs which may probably require his presence in parts beyond the Seas is desirous to render up and be discharged from the Execution of the said Trust and the other Associates are by their ffamily occasions often called to a distance from London *And Whereas* the said Doctor Thomas Bray findeth himself in a declining State of Health which he doubteth may soon disable him from performing the said Trust and the said Doctor Thomas Bray and his said Associates fearing so good and pious a Design should be dropt for want of a sufficient Number of proper persons to carry on so laudable and laborious an Undertaking find it necessary to increase the Number of their Associates *Now Know ye* that to the End Intent and purpose that the said Robert Hales may according to his Desire be legally discharged of and from Executing the said Trust and that so laudable an Undertaking may not be frustrated for want of a sufficient Number of persons proper to carry it on and that the said Legacies or Sums of Money may continue to be faithfully and honestly applied according to the true Intent and meaning of the said Testators Will The said Reverend Doctor Thomas Bray Lord Viscount Percival Robert Hales Stephen Hales and William Belitha do hereby Declare The honourable Edward Digby Esqr. The honourable Colonell George Carpenter James Oglethorpe of Westbrook Place in the County of Surrey

Esqr. The honourable Edward Harley Esqr. one of the Auditors of his Majesties Exchequer The honourable James Vernon Esqr. one of the Clerks of his Majesty's most honourable Privy Councel Edward Hughes Esqr. Judge Advocate of his Majesty's Court Martial Robert Hucks of the Parish of St. Gyles's in the ffields Esqr. Thomas Tower of the Inner Temple Esqr. Rogers Holland of Chippenham in Wilts Esqr. John Laroche of Milgate in Kent Esqr: Major Charles Selwyn of Richmond in the County of Surrey Robert More of Bishops Castle in the County of Salop Esqr. Erasmus Philips of St. Andrew Holbourne Esqr. John Campbel of St. George in the ffields in Com̃ Middlesex Esqr. James Lowther of Whitehaven Esqr. William Sloper of St. James's Esqr. - - - St. John of Soho Esqr. Henry Hastings of Westminster Esqr. Mr. Thomas Carpenter of ffriday Street - - - Smith of the - - - Temple Esqr. - - - Anderson - - - Captain Thomas Coram The Reverend Digby Cotes Principal, M. A., University Orator The Reverend Mr. Arthur Bedford The Reverend Mr. Samuel Smith Lecturer of St. Alban Woodstreet The Reverend Mr. Bundy The Reverend Mr. Richard King Vicar of Topsham in the County of Devon The Reverend John Burton M. A. their Associates or ffellow Trustees of the aforesaid Legacies or Sums of money for the Uses Intents and purposes mentioned in the said Will and therefore the said Will and therefore the said Doctor Thomas Bray and his said Associates Vizt. The Lord Viscount Percival Robert Hales Stephen Hales and William Belitha Do and each of them Doth hereby assign transfer and set over unto themselves ... and the Survivors or Survivor of them and the Assigns of such Survivor the aforesaid Legacies or Sums of Money be the same more or less given and bequeathed or ordered willed or directed to be paid or delivered unto the said Doctor Thomas Bray in and by the said recited Will and every part and parcell thereof to be applyed bestowed and employed as they ... or the major part of them or of the Survivors of them shall order direct and appoint and do further give and grant unto them the sd. Trustees and Associates to and for such Uses Intents and Purposes as are mentioned and expressed in the said Mr. D'Allones Will according to the true Intent and meaning thereof all their Right Power and Authority to act and do in the Premises as fully and amply to all Intents Constructions and purposes as the said Doctor Thomas Bray Lord Viscount Percival Stehen Hales and William Belitha might or could do therein by virtue of the said Will and before recited Deed. *And* the said Doctor Thomas Bray Lord Viscount Percival Stephen Hales and William Belitha Do by these Presents give and grant to themselves and the . . . major part of them and the Survivors of them and the major part of them full power right and Authority to elect nominate and appoint by way of Balloting any new Associate or Associates who shall and may have the like power vested in them to act in the said Trust Except to the Election of new Members which is hereby reserved to those only above mentioned *And further* that this good Work may be kept on ffoot in Case of Mortality of some of us [they] . . . do hereby for themselves severally and respectively agree when or before (as occasion shall require) the number of the Survivors of the said Associates and Trustees shall be reduced to ffive to Elect nominate and appoint other Trustees and Associates vested with the same powers right & authority. *Lastly* they do . . . and each of them for himself his Heirs Executors and Administrators doth hereby declare and make known that they will not nor any of them or the Heirs Executors and Administrators of them or any of them shall or will be answerable or accountable for the Acts Deeds Receipts Payments or Dafaults of the other of them but Each for himself and his own Acts Deeds Receipts Payments and Defaults only nor shall or will any of them respectively be answerable for any money but what shall be actually received by them respectively. *In Witness* whereof We have hereunto set our hands and Seals the ffifteenth day of January in the third year of the Reign of our Sovereign Lord George the Second of Great Brit-

ain ffrance and Ireland King Defender of the ffaith Anno Domini
One thousand Seven hundred and Twenty Nine.
      [seal] Thomas Bray
      [seal]
      [seal] Robert Hales.
      [seal] Stephen Hales
      [seal] Wm: Belitha[4]

The Minutes of the Meetings of the Trustees for Instructing of the Negroes in the Christian Religion, and Establishing a charitable Colony for the better Maintainance of the poor of this Kingdom, and for other good Purposes.[5]

At a Meeting of the Trustees for Mr D'Allone's Charity for the Instruction of the Negroes in America, on Saturday the twenty first Day of March in the year of our Lord 1729 [O.S.], there being present Mr Hales, Mr Belitha, Mr Digby, Col. Carpenter, Mr Oglethorpe, Mr Hughes Mr Hucks, Mr Towers, Mr La Roche, Mr Moor, Mr James Lowther, Mr Anderson, Arthur Bedford. The Reverend Mr Smith, Mr Bundy. Cap. Coram.

1 The new Feofment signed by Dr Bray and the other antient Feoffees was read.

2 A Proposal of Mr Oglethorpe for Applying to the Trustees for a Part of Mr Joseph King's Legacy of 15000 li for Establishing a charitable Colony for the better Maintainance of the poor of the City of London, and elsewhere within these Kingdomes was read.

3 Agreed that this Society are willing to do whatever shall be thought proper for them to promote so good a Design, and Mr Oglethorpe was desired to take such Measures, as he should think most proper for Making the same the same succesful.

4 Agreed, that an Abstract of Mr D'Allone's Will, and of what hath been done in Pursuance thereof be laid before the Society at their next Meeting in Order to be printed.

5 An Objection being raised, that the Christian Names of several of the Feoffees were omitted in the Feofment, and that the Feofment having been signed and sealed, and one of the old Feoffees being dead, nothing could be inserted therein; and that no particular Person could act by Virtue of his Sirname only being mentioned in the said Deed, because there were many Persons of the same Sirname, it is agreed to consider thereof at the next Meeting.

6 Arthur Bedford being desired to take the Books lately in the Custody of Dr Bray for the Use of the Missionaries to America into his Apartments at the Haberdasher's Hospital at Hoxton, he agreed thereto.

7 Arthur Bedford also acquainted the Society, that he had received into his Custody the Books, which Dr Bray had left by Will to be sold for fifty Pounds for the Beginning of a parochial Library in any Market Town in the Kingdom of England, containing in Number 484 Books, and placed up together in eighteen Boxes, but that he never yet had a Catalogue of them, and that he would be accountable for both Parcels, Fires, Thieves and other such like Casualties being excepted.

Adjourned until Tuesday the twenty eighth Day of April 1730

[*Percival, April 1, 1730*]

I called on Mr. Oglethorp, who kept me three hours and more in explaining his project of sending a colony of poor and honest industrious debtors to the West Indies by means of a charitable legacy left by one King, a haberdasher, to be disposed of as his executors should please. Those executors have agreed that five thousand pounds of the money shall be employed to such a purpose, and our business is to get a Patent or Charter for incorporating a number of honest and reputable persons to pursue this good work, and as those executors desired the persons entrusted with that sum might be annexed to some Trust already in being, I am desired to consent to admit such as are to manage that money into my trust for disposing of the legacy left by Mr. Dalone for converting negroes to Christianity, to which I very readily have consented, the Lord Chancellor allowing thereof, which is not to be doubted. Mr Oglethorp told me that the number relieved by the last year's Act out of prison for debt are ten thousand, and that three hundred are returned to take the benefit thereof from Prussia, many of whom are woollen manufacturers.⁶

[*Percival, April 11, 1730*]

Went to the Temple to give Mr. Annesley the deed for augmenting the number of trustees of Dalone's Legacy, which he thinks cannot be done by us five trustees originally appointed, but by the Master of the Rolls, by bill and answer.⁷

2 At a Meeting of the Trustees for Mr D'Allone's Charity for the Instruction of the Negroes in America on Tuesday the twelfth Day of May in the Year of our Lord 1730.## Mr Hales, Mr Belitha, Mr Digby, Mr Carpenter, Mr Oglethorpe, Mr Vernon, Mr Hughes, Mr Tower. Mr Holland, Mr La Roche, Mr Anderson, Capt. Coram. Mr Bundy. Mr Smith.⁸

1 A printed Epistle of Dr Bray to Mr D'Allone's Trustees was given every one of the Feoffees then present.⁹

⟨2 A Paper was signed in the Name of all the Trustees then present, and is as followeth.⟩

2 The Persons present agreed to accept of the said Trust, or Trusts and to execute the same, under the Direction of the High Court of Chancery,## and they signified their Consent by Letters.

and Mr Oglethorpe was desired to apply to the Court for that Purpose, and ⟨he was desired⟩ to give Notice, when Matters were ripe for another Meeting

Adjourned until such ⟨Time as Mr Oglethorpe shall think fit to summon them again, and he was desired to give Notice thereof when Matters were ripe for another Meeting⟩ Notice be given as aforesaid.

3 At a Meeting of the ⟨Feoffees⟩ Trustees for Mr D'Allone's Charity for the Instruction of the Negroes in America on Wednesday the first Day of July in the Year of our Lord 1730 there being present, The Right Honourable the Lord Percivall, The Reverend Mr Stephen Hales, Mr Belitha, Mr Oglethorpe, Mr Vernon, Mr Holland, Mr La Roche, Mr Heathcote, Mr Anderson, Captain Coram, The Reverend Mr Smith, Mr Bundy and Arthur Bedford.

1 A printed Epistle of Dr Bray to Mr D'Allone's Trustees was given to those Members then present, who had not before received the same.

Ordered that one of them be sent in the next Letter to each of the other ⟨Feoffees⟩ Trustees, who have not as yet received any one of them, provided it can be done without the Charge of Postage.[10]

2 Mr Oglethorpe reported that on Wednesday the twenty fourth Day of June last, the Cause concerning the Charity of Mr D'Allone, and of Dr Brays Feofment in Pursuance of the same was heard before the Master of the Rolls, who ⟨said several handsome things⟩ spoke with Respect of the new Society formed thereby, and not only promised it all the Encouragement, which lay in his Power, but also gave a final Decree, the most advantageous to the Society, which could be desired, and appointed the Gentlemen, who were Associates to Dr Bray to Act as Trustees for Executing

Mr D'Allone's Will, and Instructing the Negroes of the British Plantations in the Christian Religion.

The Minutes of the said Decree was read, and the Thanks of the Society were returned to Mr Oglethorpe for his great Care, and Advancing the Mony in that Affair.

3 Agreed, that a Chairman be chosen, to continue in that Office for one Year, and that Mr Oglethorpe be the ⟨said⟩ present Chairman.

4 Agreed, that in the Absence of the Chairman some other Person be appointed by the Majority of any Meeting, to act in his Place until he is present.

5 Agreed, that from the Beginning of any Meeting of this Society until it is adjourned, there shall be no Discourse, but such as is proper for the Affairs of this Society, and that it is the Business of the Chairman to prevent every thing that is foreign to the Purpose, ⟨and especially all trivial tumultous or private Discourse of members to one another,⟩ and that the Chairman shall direct every Person to speak in their Turns, and that all Persons shall direct their Discourse to the Chairman.

6 Agreed, that the Reverend Mr Samuel Smith and Arthur Bedford be the Secretaries to this Society, to act either joyntly or separately therein, as Occasion shall require, to continue in this Office until the first Day of February next.

7 Agreed, that it is the Business of the Reverend Mr Samuel Smith to write Letters to, and receive them from the Correspondents of this Society, and to enter those, which shall be found to be material, in a Book to be kept for that Purpose, and to communicate all such Letters to this Society ⟨, as Occasion shall require⟩.

8 Agreed, that it is the Business of Arthur Bedford to take in Writing the Minutes of each Meeting, and to transcribe them fairly in a Book against the next Meeting, to keep also a Memorandum Book of the Matters, which deserve farther Consideration to make proper Indexes for both ⟨, at the End of every Year, and

in the intermediate Time, to write all Proposals, which shall be made by any ⟨⟨Person⟩⟩ Member of this Society, for the better Promoting of the Designs, in which they are, or shall be engaged, and to communicate them, with what he himself shall think proper, to this Society at their next Meeting⟩.

9 Agreed, that the Minutes of each former Meeting be read over at the Beginning of the next, and after that the Letters, which were sent or received since the last Meeting, and that then all other Matters, which occur, be taken into Consideration, and minuted down accordingly, and that at the End of each Meeting, all the Minutes of the said Meeting be read over and signed by the Chairman.

10 Agreed that no Bargains or Contracts be made upon the same Day in which they are proposed and that this be a Standing Order.

11 Agreed, ⟨that this Society will meet once in fourteen Days, namely on Thursday at nine of the Clock in the Morning, or oftner upon Summons, as the Chairman shall think fit⟩ as Business shall happen, the Chairman ⟨shall⟩ be impowered to Summon the Society.

12 Agreed, that none of ⟨these⟩ the Standing, Orders made by this Society be at any Time repealed, except at a Meeting, when nine of the Members at the least, are actually present.

13 Arthur Bedford reported, that he, having an Occasion to wait on the Bishop of London on Munday the twenty second Day of June last,[11] took the Opportunity to communicate to his Lordship the Designs of this Society, upon which his Lordship was pleased to express his great Satisfaction therewith, and that so many very worthy Persons were concerned therein. He farther added, that he should give it all the Encouragements and Assistance, which lay in his Power, and be ready upon all Occasions to correspond with them. That he himself had printed some Tracts on this Subject, particularly an Exhortation to contribute to the said Design. And that he had also taken Care to obtain an exact List of all the

Negroes in the English Plantations in America, all which Particulars he was willing to lay before them, that so they might know how to proportion their Charity as there was Occasion.

Agreed, That Mr Vernon, Mr Oglethorpe, Mr Bundy and Arthur Bedford do wait on the Lord Bishop of London, and desire his Protection of, and Concurrence with the Designs of this Society.

14 Agreed, That this Society will endeavour to cultivate a good Understanding with the Society for the Propagating of the Gospel in foreign Parts, and that such Members of this Society as are Members of the other Society do acquaint them therewith.

15 Agreed, That this Society will endeavour to cultivate a good Understanding with the Society for Promoting Christian Knowledge, and that such Members of this Society as are Members of the other Society, do acquaint them therewith.

⟨16 Agreed, that this Society do call itself for the Future by the Name of The Trustees for Instructing the British Negroes in the Principles of the Christian Religion, and Establishing a charitable Colony for the better Maintainance of the Poor of this Kingdom, and other good Purposes.⟩

17 Agreed, that Endeavours be used as soon as possible, to obtain ⟨from the Kings most excellent Majesty⟩ a Grant of Lands ⟨for the Erecting of a Colony in Carolina⟩[12] in America, that such poor Persons may be transplanted thither, who shall be willing to go beyond the Seas for their better Maintainance, ⟨to be under the Direction and Management of this Society,⟩ and that Mr Oglethorpe, and such other Persons of this Society, whom he shall desire for his Assistance do take Care of the same.

18 Mr Smith acquainted this Society, that he had received a Letter from the Lady Betty Hastings,[13] in which she acknowledged the Receipt of a Library of fifteen Pounds Value, and was indebted five Pounds for the same, which was applied for the Use of a Clergy Man of her Acquaintance, and that she desired another Library for another Clergy Man, upon the same Terms and of the same Value.

Agreed, that Mr Smith be desired to send a Letter to the Lady Betty Hastings, to acquaint her Ladyship, that the said Library shall be sent according to her Desire, and that both the five Pounds be paid to Mr Smith.

19 Agreed, that Letters be wrote to all ⟨Clergy Men⟩ Persons in England ⟨and Wales⟩, who formerly received any Library from Dr Bray, desiring them to give a particular Account of those Libraries, and that all Correspondence with those Clergy in the American Plantations, who formerly corresponded with Dr. Bray, be renewed.

20 Agreed, that the next Meeting be on Thursday the sixteenth Day of July next, at nine of the Clock in the Morning, and that the Place be where Mr Oglethorpe shall think fit to appoint.

J. Oglethorpe.

[*Percival, July 1, 1730*]

Went to town to a meeting of the new Society for fulfilling Mr. Dalone's will in the conversion of negroes, and disposing of five thousand pounds, a charity that will be put in our hands by Mr. King's trustees, and which we design to dispose in settling some hundred of families in Carolina, who came necessitous out of gaols by virtue of our late debtors Act.[14]

At a Meeting of the Trustees for Instructing of the Negroes in the Christian Religion, ⟨and Establishing a charitable Colony for the better Maintainance of the poor of this Kingdom,⟩ and for other good Purposes on Wednesday the fifteenth Day of July, at Manwaring's Coffee House, at nine of the Clock in the Morning, there being present. the Right honourable the Lord Percivall, The Reverend Mr Stephen Hales, Mr Digby, Colonel Carpenter, Mr Oglethorpe, Mr Vernon, Mr Heathcote,

Mr Anderson, Captain Coram, The Reverend Mr Bundy, Mr Smith, and Arthur Bedford.[15]

1 Mr Oglethorpe reported, that he had received the Summe of twenty Pounds to be paid to the Trustees from a Person, who desires to be unknown to be applied for the Benefit of the Charitable Colony.

Agreed, that the Thanks of the Trustees be given to the said Benefactor by Mr Oglethorpe.

2 Mr Hales reported, that he had received five Guineas from Mr Belitha to be applied for the Designs of the Society in General.

Agreed, that the Thanks of the Trustees be given to Mr Belitha by Mr Hales.

Agreed, that the said Summes of twenty five Pounds and five Shillings be kept in the Hands of Mr Oglethorpe until farther Orders.

3 Mr Oglethorpe, Mr Vernon, Mr Bundy and Arthur Bedford reported, that they had according to Order waited ⟨upon⟩ on the Bishop of London, that his Lordship thanked the Society for their Messages, that he was very ready to give them all Countenance, Encouragement and Assistance in Carrying on their good Designs, and desired to know the Methods, in which they intended to proceed.

Agreed, that Mr Oglethorpe, Mr Huckes, Mr Bundy and Mr Smith. be desired to wait ⟨upon⟩ on the Bishop of London, to thank his Lordship for the favourable disposition expressed by him toward ⟨the Designs of⟩ this Society, and ⟨to⟩ that they do acquaint him, ⟨that in the present Circumstances⟩ that the Method ⟨of Pursuing Dr Brays Intentions which effectually will be⟩, which appears to them the most effectual of Pursuing Dr Brays Intentions, is in their present Circumstances, ⟨by continuing to send⟩ that of sending Books to the Missionaries in the Manner which the Dr himself did, thereby to enable and encourage them to undertake the Conversion of the Negroes, within their respective Parishes.

4 Agreed, that the Society do at their next Meeting consider of a Method of sending a Parochial Library into the Highlands of Scotland.
Adjourned to Thursday the 30th Instant, at 9 of the Clock.
James Oglethorpe

5 At a Meeting of the Trustees for Instructing of the Negroes in the Christian Religion, and for other good Purposes on Thursday the thirtieth Day of July, at Manwaring's Coffee House, at nine of the Clock in the Morning, there being present. The Lord Percival, Mr Oglethorpe, Mr Huckes, Mr Smith, Captain Coram, Mr Hales, Mr Vernon, Mr Towers, Mr Anderson, and Arthur Bedford.

⟨1 Mr Oglethorpe reported, that he had received the Summe of twenty Pounds from - - - to be paid to the Trustees, and applied for the Benefit of the Charitable Colony.⟩

⟨Agreed, that the Thanks of the Trustees be given to the said Benefactor by Mr Oglethorpe.⟩

2 Agreed, that a Memorandum Book be kept, and that the Particulars inserted therein, which remain to be considered, be read on the first Day of February yearly.

3 Arthur Bedford reported, that the Books, which were lately in the Custody of Dr. Bray for the Use of Parochial Libraries, and the Missionaries into America, were brought into his Apartments, on Tuesday the twenty fourth Day of March last, consisting of a Cart Load, and that they are all in his Custody at this Time, except a Library, which was given to the Reverend Mr John Fulton, a Missionary into South Carolina,[16] on the sixth Day of April last, and that he had digested them into a Catalogue, by which it might be known, whether any particular Book was there or not, and how many there were of each Sort, and they were so placed, that Recourse might be had to any Book upon any particular Occasion,

which Catalogue was produced, and the Method appeared to be satisfactory to this Society.

4 Agreed, that this Society will heartily concur in any other Method, which shall be proposed, whereby the Glory of God, and a true sense of Religion may be promoted in this, or in any other Part of His Majesties Dominions.

5 Agreed, that printed Letters be sent to each Trustee, who lives within the ⟨ - - - Miles⟩ the Limits of the Limits of [sic] the ⟨City of London⟩ Peny Post ⟨ - - - Days before each Meeting⟩, to give them Notice thereof, and that the Letters be sent by the Peny Post, and by the Secretary, and that as soon as this Society is regulated, Notice of the Time and Place of these Meetings shall be sent by a Letter to all other Members, that they may be present, whenever they shall think fit, if they shall happen to come to London. Ad Deliberandu[m]

6 Agreed, that each Member leaves with the Society sufficient Instructions, where any Letter may be directed to him, and that he always doth the same, whenever new Directions shall happen to be necessary.

The present Directions are these.

✓ For the Right honourable John Lord Viscount Percivall, at his House in Charleton[17]

✓ For the Reverend Mr Stephen Hales at his House in Teddington near Hampton Court.

✓ For William Belitha Esq at his House at Kingston upon Thames

✓ For the Honourable Edward Digby Esq at his House at his house [sic] in Clargis [Clarges] Street.

✓ For the Honourable George Carpenter at his House at Bond Street.

For ⟨the Worshipful⟩ James Oglethorpe Esq at his House in the Old Palace Yard in Westminster.

✓ For Auditor Edward Harley Esq, at his Chambers in Lincoln's Inn.

✓ For the Honourable James Vernon Esq at his House in Grosvenor Street.

✓ For Edward Hughes Esq Member at the Horse Guards.

✓ For Robert Hucks. Esq at his House in Great Russell Street

✓ For ⟨ John⟩ Thomas Tower⟨s⟩ Esq at his Chambers in the Temple

✓ For Rogers Holland Esq at his Chambers in the Temple.

✓ For John La Roche Esq at his House in Pall' Mall.

✓ For Major Charles Selwyn, Member of Parliament at his House in Richmond.

✓ For Robert More Esq at his Lodgings in York Buildings.

✓ For William Sloper at his ⟨Chambers⟩ Park Place in St James's Place.

For Oliver St John Esq at his House in Soho Square.[18]

For Henry Hastings, Esq

✓ For George Heathcott. Esq at his House in Soho Square.

✓ For Francis Eyles, at Mr Heathcott's Ditto

✓ For Adam Anderson, at his House in Red lion Street near Clerkenwell Green.

✓ For Sr. James Lowther, at his House in Queen Square.

⟨For Erasmus Philips Esq⟩

✓ For Captain Thomas Coram at his House in Prescott Street in Goodman's Fields.

For the Reverend Digby Cotes ⟨Esq President⟩ Principall of Magdalen Hall in Oxford.

✓ For Arthur Bedford at the Haberdasher's Hospital at Hoxton.

✓ For the Reverend Mr Samuel Smith, at Mr Bentham's House near Aldgate Church

✓ For the Reverend Mr Richard Bundy at King's Square Court, near Soho Square.

For the Reverend Mr John Burton, at his Chambers in Corpus Christi College in Oxford.

For the Reverend Mr Daniel Somerscald Vicar of Dodington near Feversham in Kent.

7 Agreed, that whoever is a Benefactor or Subscriber, shall have the Liberty at any Time, either of Leaving his Subscription at large, for the Designs of the Trustees in general, or of Appropriating the same to any Branch thereof, and every Benefactor shall have free Access to the Books ⟨, and Leave to be present at all Debates⟩.

⟨8 A Petition to the Kings most excellent Majesty, desiring a Grant of certain Lands in America for the better Maintainance of the Poor of this Kingdom, was read, and signed by the Members then present.⟩

⟨Agreed, that it be signed by all the other Members as soon as possible, and presented to His Majesty, and after that, that it be entered in the Book of Letters.⟩

9 Arthur Bedford reported, that on Sunday the twelfth Day of this Month, Mr Gardiner acquainted him, that there was a Cart Load of Books at Mr Newman's House in Bartlett's Buildings, and about two Hundred at Mr Cholmley's a Bookbinder in the Strand, which were given for Parochial Libraries, the Property whereof was vested in himself, and the Reverend Mr Fox of Reading,[19] that he was willing to dispose of his Right therein, provided he had a Catalogue of them, an Account, where they were lodged, and a Promise of Disposing of them, as soon as it was convenient, and that he might have an Account from Time to Time, how they were disposed of, and that a Library to the Value of twenty Pounds might be sent to a poor Living in Wiltshire, which Mr Fox should recommend, and that he did not doubt, but Mr Fox would readily agree to the same.

Accordingly a Letter was sent to Mr Fox, the Copy whereof was read, with the Answer to the same, which had been also communicated to Mr Gardiner on this Day.

Agreed, that Arthur Bedford do take the most proper Method

with Mr Fox, Mr Gardiner and the Society for Promoting Christian Knowledge, that the Books may be had as soon as possible for this Society upon the Terms mentioned by Mr Fox in the same Letter. Ad Deliberandum, and that Care be taken concerning the State of the Prisons

⟨10 Mr Bundy reported, that he had communicated to the Society for the Propagating of Christian Knowledge in foreign Parts, the Design of these Trustees to cultivate a good Understanding with them, and that - - - ⟩

11 Mr Anderson being well acquainted with the Methods of the South Sea Company, acquainted the Trustees by a Note in Writing, that these following Paper Books were wanting to carry on their Designs in the most regular Manner,

First. A rough Minute Book of four Quires *Medium*, in green Buckram, with a red Line two Inches from the left Hand.

Secondly, A fair Minute Book five Quires, *Demy* in green Vellum, with a red Line, three Inches from the Left Hand, (or rather two red Lines a Quarter of an Inch asunder, to mark in Figures the Number of the Minute) the said three Inch Margin to be for Writing in Words against each Minute respectively *D'allone's Charity* - - - *New Colony* - - - *Parochial Libraries*. - - - Before this Book there must be first a large Alphabet, whereby any particular Minute may be easily found. Secondly. An Index for each of the three Branches above mentioned, containing the Folio, where every Minute of each Branch may be found.

Thirdly, A Ledger Book of three Quires, Royal Paper, ruled as usual, for Raising the Heads of - - - *Stock*. - - - *Cash* - - - *Books*, - - - *Provisions* - - - *Ammunition* - - - *Incident-Charges &c* - - - in such a Manner, that on the Creditor or Right Hand Side of Stock Account, should be found all Receipts, Donations &c. and on the Debtor Side thereof all Issuings, Payments and Charges whatsoever, (only the Treasurer should in his Pocket Book keep a whole Months Account of Disbursements to be entered in one Article on the Creditor Side of the Stock) this Book to be divided by two Leaves of blue Paper. between each Quire, for each of the Branches distinctly, in such a Manner, that when full they may be separately bound up and an Alphabet to each.

Fourthly, A Book for Registering all Manner of Papers for each Branch, 4 Quires *Medium* with a three Inch Margin, to the three first Parts, each Quire divided as the last Book, in Case of being bound up separately, and an Alphabetical Index to each Part. The last Book to be divided into Columns. The first containing the Number prefix'd to each Book in the Catalogue, for Parochial Libraries. The second containing the Number of Books in the preceding Numbers. And the rest having on the Head thereof the Day of the Month when any Books were delivered out for Parochial Libraries, and in the common Meeting of the respective Squares, which shall be ruled accordingly, there shall be inserted the Number of the said Books so disposed of at such a Time.

Fifthly, A Book of Letters, ruled, indexed and partitioned as above ⟨, unless it be thought distinct enough to register the said Letters in the beforementioned Book with the other Papers⟩.

Agreed, that said—Books be bought ⟨unruled⟩ for the said Purpose, and that Mr Anderson be desired do [to] take Care thereof, and that afterward Mr Anderson be desired to assist the Secretary in Settling the said Books and Indexes in the Method by him mentioned.

12 Agreed, that a Book Box be bought for the better keeping together the said Books and other Papers, and Deeds, and that Arthur Bedford—do take Care thereof ⟨, and that the said Box be kept in the Closet adjoyning to the Room where the Trustees do meet, and that the Key be sealed up in a Paper at the End of every Meeting when it is called for and be kept by the Landlord of the House, to be produced, as Occasion shall require⟩.

⟨13 Agreed, that there be four Meetings of the Trustees, the first to be on Thursday the - - - Day of - - - to settle all Matters relating to Mr D'allone's Charity, the second to be on Thursday the - - - Day of - - - to settle all Matters relating to the Charitable

Colony. The third to be on Thursday the - - - Day of - - - to settle all Matters relating to parochial Libraries, and the fourth to be on Thursday the - - - Day of - - - to read over all such Deeds, Wills, and other Papers, which shall be thought proper to be inserted in the Book to be kept for that Purpose, and that the Secretary give Notice to each Member of the particular Design of such Meetings. But when the particular Business of each Meeting is ended, the Trustees may, if they think proper, proceed on any other Branch of their Designs.⟩

⟨14 Agreed, that the Trustees will also furnish the Clergy in Wales with parocial Libraries according to their Ability, when Occasion shall require.⟩

15 Agreed, that printed Copies of Dr Brays Letter to Mr D'allone's Trustees be sent to those Members, who have not yet received them, as soon as it can conveniently be done without the Charge of Postage. The Persons, who have not as yet received them are Mr Sloper, Mr St. John, Mr Hastings, Mr Eyles, Mr Cotes, Mr Burton, and Mr Somerschald. ⟨ and Mr Philips⟩[20]

16 Mr Oglethorpe reported that of Friday last being the 24th Instant Mr Huckes, Mr Bundy and Mr Smith - - - had waited on the Lord Bishop of London in Pursuance of the Direction of the Trustees at the last Meeting, and that his Lordship thanked the Society, and as for the rest he referred himself to Mr Bundy.

⟨17 The Society proceeding to take into Consideration the Method of sending a Parochial Library into the Highlands of Scotland it is agreed, that - - - ⟩

18 A Letter to and another from Mr Fox concerning Books given to Parochial Libraries were read,

Agreed, that Arthur Bedford write a full Answer thereto, and acquaint Mr Fox, that the Trustees will send ⟨two Libraries⟩ a 15 li Library to the Place ⟨which he recommends⟩ of his Appointment, as soon as conveniently they can, and give him a particular Account thereof after they are sent, upon the Terms prescribed by Dr Bray, and in the Act of Parliament.[21]

19 A Letter from the Reverend Mr Price,[22] and another to him concerning a Method for a Clergy Man in his Studies was read.

Agreed that they are kept with the other Letters. ⟨Ad Consid:⟩ July 30th. 1730.

20 Mr Vernon laid a Draught of a Petition to the King, for the Grant of certain Lands to the Southward of Carolina. Agreed that Thanks be returned to Mr Vernon for his Care.

Agreed that the Petition be engrossed and signed.

21 Mr Hales paid to the Society 5 li.5s. from Mr Belitha, to the Designs in General,

Agreed, that Mr Hales return him Thanks for the same.

Mr Hales gave 3l. 3s. of his own for the Designs in general, and thanks were returned to him for the same.

22 Mr Smith paid 5li. 5s from the Lady Betty Hastings for the Use of parochial Libraries,

Agreed, that Mr Smith return her Ladyship Thanks for the same.

23 The Lord Percival acquainted the Associates, that Colonel Schutz had presented them ten Guineas out of the Princes Charity for the Conversion of the Negroes,[23] and Furtherance of the intended Colony,

Agreed, that Thanks be returned to Colonel Schutz by The Lord Percival for the same.

24 Mr Oglethorpe acquainted the Associates, that he had received 20li from a Person who desires to be unknown, for the intended Colony.

Agreed, that Mr Oglethorpe return Thanks for the same to the said Benefactor

25 Mr Oglethorpe reported, that the Subgovenours and Directors of the Royal African Company had desired him to acquaint the Associates, that they intend to be Benefactors to them, for Promoting their Designs, and that they have written to Cape Coast Castle,[24] to inquire into the State of the Library sent thither by Dr Thomas Bray deceased.

26 Agreed, that the Reverend Mr Smith and Arthur Bedford do make out a List of a 15li Library and incidental Charges, to be laid before the Associates at their next Meeting.

27 A Copy of a Letter from Mr Smith to the Occupiers of Parochial Libraries was read, and agreed to be sent to the Parties concerned.

28 Agreed, that the Days of Meeting be on the second and fourth Thursdays on every Month.

Agreed That the Thanks of The associates be given to the Red: Ar: Bedford for the great diligence & zeal he hath show'd in digesting the books given by Dr Bray in to a Catalogue.[25]

James Oglethorpe

#At a Meeting of the Society for the Propagation of the Gospel into foreign Parts 17th July 1730.

The Reverend Mr Bundy acquainted the Board, That the Trustees appointed by the Court of Chancery for the Application of Mr D'allone's Legacy for the Conversion of the Negroes in the foreign Plantations and other good Purposes are desirous to keep up a good Correspondence with the Society in Order to promote the Instruction of the Negroes. Agreed that Mr Bundy be desired to return the Thanks of this Society to the said Trustees, and acquaint them, that this Society is very ready to promote the good Design they are engaged in, and to give them all the Assistance they can,

David Humpris
Secretary.[26]

[*Percival, July 30, 1730*]

We agreed on a petition to the King and Council for obtaining a grant of lands on the south-west of Carolina for settling poor persons of London, and having ordered it be to engrossed fair, we signed it, all who were present, and the other Associates were to be spoke also to sign it before delivered. A paper drawn up for Captain Coram to carry to Tunbridge in order to collect subscriptions to our scheme, conditional that a grant be made us of lands desired, was showed me, and my leave desired that I might be mentioned in it, because they thought it might facilitate subscriptions, and I readily gave it, but advised that some others might likewise be mentioned in it. . . .

. . . .

Friday, 31.—Went by appointment with Mr Oglethorp to see Mr. Carpenter, one of the three Trustees of Mr. King's Charity, from whom we expect five thousand pounds for the settlement of our colony. He was well disposed, but some had been tampering with him to make him believe that disposal of the charity money was not suitable to the deceased's will. We came away and resolved that Councillor Mead's opinion thereupon should be asked to satisfy Mr. Carpenter. One Smith and Gordon are the other trustees of that charity.[27]

[*The King's Privy Council, September 17, 1730*]

{Reference to a Committee of the petition of Viscount Perceval, the Hon. Edward Digby and others} praying His Majesty to Grant them a Tract of Lands in South Carolina lying between the River Savana and Alortamalla in order to Establish a Charitable Colony thereon, and likewise to Grant them a Charter of Incorporation whereby they may be enabled to enter into Contract with such Familys as are willing to settle there, and to receive Charitable Benefactions of all those who are willing to promote the said Undertaking.[28]

At a Meeting of the Associates for Mr Dallone's Charity at Manwaring's Coffee House, on Friday the second Day of October Anno 1730, at twelve of the Clock, there being

Present. Mr Oglethorpe, Mr Vernon, Captain Coram, Mr Anderson and Arthur Bedford. Mr Hughes

Mr Bundy acquainted the Associates that he had laid before the Society for Propagating the Gospel into Foreign Parts, that these Associates desired to cultivate a good Understanding with them, and that they had desired him to return their Answer, which he delivered in Writing, and is as follows.*

Several Letters were read relating to Parochial Libraries, and it is agreed that a Committee be appointed ⟨considering⟩ to consider all Letters, and Matters relating to Parochial Libraries, and that Mr Bundy, Mr Smith, Mr Hales, Arthur Bedford, and any other Members, who shall be willing to come, be of the said Committee, and that their first Meeting be at Manwaring's Coffee, and that their first Meeting be on Thursday Oct. 15, at half an Hour after twelve of the Clock.

Mr Vernon ⟨reported to⟩ laid before the Associates, that the supposed Insurrections of the Negroes in Virginia and in the other Plantations in America had occasioned several Reflections on the Designs of these Associates, and it being proposed that the best Methods of Preventing the Effects thereof would be in the first Place to inquire into the Truth of the Facts, and the Assistance of each Associate in their several Stations be desired for this Purpose, that Mr Smith write to his Correspondents in America on this Subject, and that Mr Bundy desires that the Society for Propagating the Gospel into foreign Parts will be pleased to do the same, the same was agreed to.

Agreed that the next Meeting be on the second ⟨Munday⟩ Thursday in November, or sooner upon Notice given if Occasion shall require

James Oglethorpe

☙ At a Meeting of the Associates for Mr Dallone's Charity for Converting the Negroes in America, and for other good Purposes at Manwarings Coffee House on Thursday the twelfth Day of November Anno 1730 at nine of the Clock in the Morning, Mr Heathcote in the Chair in the Absence of Mr Oglethorpe there being also present Mr Towers, Mr Huckes, Mr La Roche, Mr Hales, Mr Smith, Mr Anderson, Captain Coram, and Arthur Bedford.

Mr Fox his Answer to a Letter concerning Parochial Libraries and Prisons, Num. 2. with an Answer to the same, Num. 3. and his Reply to the Answer granting the Books in his and Mr. Gardiner's Custody to these Associates for the Use of Parochial Libraries, Num. 4, and a Letter to Archdeacon Frank for Settling a Library in Stretly Parish in Bedford Shire,[29] Num. 5, and a Letter sent with Dr Bray's printed Letter to Mr D'allone's Trustees, Num. 8, were read.

1 Agreed, that an Answer of Thanks be returned to Mr Fox, and that he be assured, that a due Care shall be taken with all possible Speed to dispose of the Books for his Satisfaction, and an Account thereof shall be kept, to be laid before Mr Gardiner and himself, whenever they shall desire it.

2 Agreed, that the Thanks of the Trustees be given to Mr Gardiner by Arthur Bedford, for his ready Compliance with Mr Fox in this Affair.

3 Arthur Bedford reported, that Mr Fox came from Reading to be present at a Meeting of these Associates on Thursday, October the 22d, being the fourth Thursday of the Month; But there being no Meeting on that Day, he acquainted the said Arthur Bedford, that one thing, which he intended to have proposed, was, that since he and Mr Gardiner had agreed, that these Associates should be intituled to all the Books vested in them for Parochial Libraries, except six Books particularly mentioned, which he found to be only in Quires, that he would take it as a Favour, if these Associates would bind them before they were sent to him at their own Charges, and that they might be sent by the Reading Coach, which

lodges at the White Horse in Fleet Street on a Munday, Wednesday or Friday Night, whose Coachman's Name is Lovegrove, and the said Arthur Bedford having such Books ready bound in his Custody upon the Account of Dr Bray lately deceased, and a Motion being made, that six of the said Books be sent to Mr Fox, according to his Desire, it passed in the Affirmative.

Agreed, That six more Books of the same Sort be bound, and paid for, out of the Lady Betty Hastings her Money to be placed in the Room of the others.

4 Agreed, That Arthur Bedford do take the Books into his Apartments, which were left by Mr Fox and Mr Gardiner in Mr Newman's Hands, with all convenient Speed, and make a Catalogue of them, to be laid before these Associates.

5 Agreed, That Arthur Bedford do take a Catalogue of the Books, which are left by Mr Fox and Mr Gardiner in Mr Cholmley the Book Binder's Hands in Bennet Court, over against the Fountain Tavern in the Strand to be laid before these Associates, and that he take Directions from them concerning the Binding of the said Books, and take such Books into his Apartments when bound, and that these two Affairs be referred to the said Arthur Bedford.

6 Agreed, That the Committee to whom all Matters and Letters relating to Parochial Libraries are referred, do meet on Munday the thirtieth Day of November, at nine of the Clock in the Morning.

7 Three Copies of Parochial Libraries of fifteen Pounds Value each being prepared by Arthur Bedford and Mr Smith to be laid before these Associates, according to an Order of the thirtieth of July last, it is agreed, that the same be referred to the said Committee.

8 Agreed, that the same Committee do also consider of Sending a Parochial Library to Colern in Wiltshire, another to Stretly in Bedford Shire, and a third to How in Norfolk Shire at the Request of the Lady Betty Hastings,[30] and report their Opinion hereon to these Associates at their next Meeting.

9 A Letter sent to the Reverend Mr Smith from Mr Holt of Barbadoes,[31] dated May 28. 1730. His Letters relating to the Parochial Libraries were referred to the Committee appointed for that Purpose.

10 The last Paragraph of the last Meeting of these Associates on the second Day of October being taken into Consideration, it appeared, that there had been no Insurrection of the Negroes in Virginia, and that the Insurrection in Jamaica was not in the least occasioned either by Instructing of them,[32] or by any Design of Instructing them in the Christian Religion; so that the Reflexions, occasioned thereby on these Associates or their Designs, were utterly false, and ought to be so far from Discouraging them, that it ought rather to induce them to go on with greater Diligence and Vigour for the Converting of these poor Souls to Christianity, especially since a Letter sent to Mr Smith dated at Barbadoes May 28, 1730 from the Reverend Mr Holt, gives great Hopes of Success.

11 Arthur Bedford reported from the Society for Promoting Christian Knowledge, that on Thursday the sixth Day of August last, they received from their Committee a Report, that these Associates desired to cultivate a good Understanding with them, upon which they unanimously resolved, that he the said Arthur Bedford do return the Thanks of that Society to these Associates for the same; and acquaint them, that they shall always endeavour, and esteem it as a great Happiness to cultivate a good Understanding with these Associates according to their Desire.

12 Arthur Bedford also acquainted these Associates, that the five Paper Books, which were ordered to be bought for the Use of these Associates, were bought of Major Hatley since deceased,[33] and were sent to his Apartments, and that the Price of them was 4li. 8s. 6d, as appeared by a Note, and that he had also bought of Mr Breye the Carpenter a Box for Books and Letters, the Price whereof was fifteen Shillings the Locks and Hinges being as good as could be bought, and that he had received Mony from Mr Ogle-

thorpe for the Payment of the same, which he did accordingly and took Receipts for that Purpose.

13 Agreed, that Mr Anderson do assist Arthur Bedford in the Settling of the Paper Books according to their intended Method, as soon as they shall have received Directions from this Society for that Purpose.

14 It being reported, that Mr Carpenter, Mr Smith and Mr Gordon the Executors of Mr Joseph King deceased could not agree in the Schemes of Settling the Charities mentioned in his Will, and that this Affair is now depending in the High Court of Chancery, it is the Opinion of these Associates, that the said Court be applied to in the most effectual Manner to oblige the said Executors to bring in their separate Schemes, that the same may be settled by the Court, and that Mr Oglethorpe be acquainted therewith.

15 The Keeping of the Keys for the Book Box and Box of Letters being taken into Consideration, and a Motion being made, that they be sealed up and left with Mr Bernard Lintott Bookseller near Temple Gate to be produced in the same Manner at every Meeting of these Associates,[34] or any of their Committees, the same was referred to the Consideration of some other Meeting.

16 It being reported, that Dr Bray in his Life Time intended to give a Book intituled Apparatus Biblicus in two Volumes in Octavo to Mrs Martin his Executrix,[35] that he had actually given one of the Volumes, and that the other was in the Store Room, and a Motion being made, that the other Volume be given to the said Mrs Martin, it passed in the Affirmative.

17 Agreed, That printed Letters be sent to each Associate, who lives either within or ten Miles Distance from London, or within the Limits of the Peny Post, and also to each Member of Parliament, who lives within twenty Miles of the City of London, five Days before each Meeting, and that the said Letters be sent by the Peny Post by the Secretary, and worded in this Manner,

Sir

The Gentlemen associated for Executing Mr D'allone's Will by Instructing the Negroe's of the British Plantations in the Christian Religion, and for Establishing a Charitable Colony in America, for Settling Parochial Libraries in great Britain, and for other good Purposes, meet on Thursday next at nine of the Clock in the Morning at Manwaring's Coffee House near St Dunstan's Church in Fleet Street, where you are desired to be present, I am

Subscribing Place and   Your humble Servant,
Time - - - 173 - - -   Subscribing the Name,

18 A Proposal of Mr Fox, that a Parliamentary Care be taken for the Constant Performance of divine Service in all the County Goals of this Kingdom being laid before these Associates, it is agreed that a Minute thereof be entered in the Memorandum Book to be farther considered, when a fit Opportunity shall present.

19 Agreed, that a Day be appointed at the next Meeting of these Associates to read over the Deeds and Papers, which are intended to be transferred into the Book bought for that Purpose, and that Notice be given in the printed Letter of the particular Design of that Meeting.

20 It being referred to this Meeting to consider of a Method for Sending a Parochial Library into the High Lands of Scotland, it is agreed, that the Fund for this Purpose being very small, these Associates cannot do it at present, But that they shall be very ready and desirous to cultivate a good Understanding with the Society for Promoting of Christian Knowledge in those Parts, and that Mr Anderson do acquaint them with the latter Part of this Resolution.

21 It being reported, that there are twelve hundred Books in Spittle Fields unbound, intituled Erasmus his Ecclesiastes,[36] and that Dr. Bray had a Property in them to Value of eighty Pounds, except the Value of those Books, which he had taken from thence,

and disposed of in his Life Time. And that the Design of Dr Bray was, that one of these Books should be given to every Library in Oxford and Cambridge, another should be lent to each Tutor, and as many more as should be thought proper for the Tutors to lend to their Pupils, that by Reading of them they may be sensible of the Weight and Duty of the Pastoral Care, before they entered into holy Orders; and that for this End the Tutors should examine their Pupils therein, as Occasion did require. It being also reported, that the Design was generally approved of in the said Universities; and a Motion being made, that some of the said Books be bound, and sent to the Universities, the same was referred to the Consideration of another Meeting. And that there be laid before them an Account of the Number of Books vested in Dr Bray, the Charge of Binding, and what Mony there is in the Hands of these Associates, which can properly be applied for this Purpose.

A Motion being made, that the Universities of Scotland be included in the same Design, it was referred to the Consideration of another Meeting.

A Motion being made, that the University of Dublin in Ireland be included in the same Design, it was referred to the Consideration of another Meeting.

22 Agreed, That some Catalogues of the Books given by Dr Bray to be sold for fifty Pounds, to begin a Library in any Market Town be transcribed, to be shown to such Persons, as may probably buy them for that Purpose, and that one of these be left with the Society for Promoting Christian Knowledge, for their Perusal, and another be left for the Perusal of these Associates, and that for this End Mr Smith do procure the said Catalogue from Mrs Martin; and that Mr Hales do send the Catalogue in his Custody to Arthur Bedford.

23 It having been proposed, that Application be made for two Parliamentary Clauses be added to some Act relating to Parochial Libraries, viz, one to settle twenty Pounds for this Purpose on every Living to be augmented by the late Queen Anne's Bounty

out of the first Profits of the said Augmentation;[37] And the other, That whoever will leave any Number of Books to any Parish not exceeding the Value of one and twenty Pounds, the Books and Prizes to be approved of in a proper Manner, his Executor shall receive two thirds of the Mony from the next Incumbent. And the Executor of the said the next Incumbent shall also receive of his Successor one half of the Mony which he thus paid to the Executor of the first. And the Books shall then remain as a Parochial Library for ever, and a Motion being made, that the same be entered in the Memorandum Book, it is agreed, that it be referred to the Committee for Parochial Libraries.

24 Agreed, that a Treatise be drawn up in Order to be printed, to encourage all Persons charitably inclined to contribute toward the Design of Mr D'allone for Instructing the Negroes of the British Plantations in the Christian Religion, and that Arthur Bedford do prepare the same.

25 Agreed, That a Treatise be drawn up in Order to be printed, to encourage all charitable Persons to contribute towards the charitable Colony intended to be fixed in some one of the American Plantations belonging to the King of Great Britain, and that Mr Oglethorpe do prepare the same.

26 Agreed, that a Treatise be drawn up in Order to be printed, to encourage all charitable Persons to contribute toward Parochial Libraries, and that Arthur Bedford do prepare the same.

27 Agreed, That it be a standing Rule, that any Book drawn up by Order of these Associates to be printed be first perused by four Members successively, to be nominated by them at four Meetings, who are to make their Report of the same, and such Amendments as they shall think proper, and that afterward the Book and Amendments be approved of or rejected by Balloting.

28 Agreed, that there be a Meeting of these Associates on the first Day of February every Year, when they shall chuse such new Associates as shall be proposed by Balloting, and that a Balloting Box be bought for that Purpose.

29 Agreed, That the Name of each Person proposed shall be mentioned to these Associates, and entered down in their Minutes on or before the first Meeting in December, and their Names shall be mentioned at each future Meeting, that the present Associates may have Time and Opportunity to inform themselves and others of the Character, of such as shall be proposed.

30 It being proposed, that a Sermon be preached on the first Day of February concerning the Instruction of the Negroes in the Christian Religion, the Consideration thereof is referred to the first Meeting, which shall be in January next.

31 It being proposed, that after Sermon there be a Dinner, the Charges thereof to be as an Ordinary, and that the Expenses shall be born by those, who shall be then present, the Consideration thereof is referred to the same Meeting.

32 It being proposed, that an Abstract of the Minutes for the whole preceding Year to be first approved of at a Meeting of these Associates, be then read over by those, who shall be present, the Consideration thereof is referred to the same Meeting.

33 It being proposed, that the Accounts be audited and setled before the said first Day of February, and that on that Day a Treasurer or Treasurers shall be chosen for the Year ensuing, the Consideration thereof is also referred to the same Meeting.

34 A new Impression of Mr Blairs Sermons on the fifth, sixth and seventh Chapters of St Matthew being proposed,[38] the Consideration thereof is referred to some other Meeting.

Adjourned to Thursday the twenty sixth Day of November next.

Geo: Heathcote

[*Committee of the Privy Council, November 23, 1730*]

By a Committee of the Lords of His Majestys most Honoble Privy Council

His Majesty having been pleased by His Order in Council of

the 17th of September last to referr unto this Committee The Humble Petition of the Right Honourable the Lord Viscount Percival the Honoble Edward Digby and severall others whose Names are thereto Subscribed, Setting forth that the Citys of London and Westminster and parts adjacent do abound with great Numbers of Indigent persons, who are reduced to such necessitys, as to become burthensome to the Publick and who would be willing to seek a Livelyhood in any of His Majestys Plantations in America, if they were provided with a Passage, and means of settling there; And humbly proposing to Undertake the trouble and Charge of transporting all such poor persons and Familys provided they may obtain a Grant of Lands in South Carolina for that purpose, together with such Powers as shall enable them to contract with persons inclinable to Settle there, And to receive the Charitable Contributions and benefactions of all such persons as are willing to encourage so good a design The Lords of the Committee this day took the said Petition into their Consideration And are thereupon pleased to Order that a Copy thereof (which is hereunto annexed) Be and it is hereby referred to the Lords Commissioners for Trade and Plantations to consider of what is therein proposed and of the properest Methods to render the same of most Service to the Publick And make Report thereof to this Committee as soon as conveniently they can.

Ja. Vernon.

To the Kings most Excellent Majesty in Council

The humble Petition of the Right Honoble the Lord Viscount Percival, the Honoble Edwd. Digby the Honoble George Carpenter, James Oglethorpe, George Heathcote, Thomas Tower, Robert More, Robert Hucks, Rogers Holland, William Sloper, Francis Eyles, John Laroche, James Vernon, William Belitha Esqrs. The Reverend Mr Stephen Hales, John Burton, Richard Bundy, Arthur

Bedford and Samuel Smith—Mr Adam Anderson and Thomas Coram—

Humbly Sheweth

That the Citys of London and Westminster and parts adjacent abound with great Numbers of Indigent Persons who are reduced to such necessitys as to become burthensome to the Public, and who would be willing to seek a livelyhood in any of Your Majestys Plantations in America if they were provided with a Passage and means of Settling there.

That your Petitioners being desirous of promoting an Undertaking so beneficiall to the Publick and well Assured of Considerable Contributions for carrying on the same Do humbly represent to Your Majesty that they are willing to undertake the trouble and Charge of transporting such poor Persons and Familys Provided they may obtain a Grant of Lands Sufficient for that purpose together with such powers as shall enable them to contract with Persons inclinable to Settle in America and to receive the Charitable Contributions and Benefactions of all such Persons as are willing to encourage so good a Design.

And We further humbly represent to Your Majesty that great Tracts of Land within the Limits of South Carolina are by the Agreement between Your Majesty and the late Proprietors of that Province vested in Your Majesty and that on the Southern part of the said Province the whole Tract of Land between the River Savanna and Alatamaha hath been hitherto unsettled by reason of Oppositions given to them from their Indian and other Neighbours And that it would be of great Service to Your Majestys Province of South Carolina and in some measure to all your Majestys Plantations on the Continent to which this Province is a Southern Frontier that there should be such a Settlement on the said Lands as would be Capable of defending themselves against any Invasions.

And by being a Barrier to South Carolina will Occasion the

taking up and Settling many hundred Thousands of Acres of Your Majestys Land lying between the said proposed Settlement on the River Savana and Charles Town which for want of such Protection have hitherto remained Wast and uncultivated and in particular that large and fruitfull Tract called the Yamesee Lands.

The premises therefore Considered Your Petitioners humbly pray that Your Majesty would be pleased to Grant them the said Tract of Land for the aforesaid Purposes and also Your Royal Charter of Incorporation where by they may be enabled to enter into Contract with such Familys as will settle thereon and to receive the Charitable Benefactions of all such Persons as are desirous to promote so good a Work And likewise to be enabled to form such By Laws as will be necessary for the well Ordering of the said intended Colony.

And your Petitioners shall ever pray &c.

Percival	James Oglethorpe	Thomas Coram
Robt: Hucks	Arthur Bedford	Samuel Smith
Stephen Hales	John Laroche	A Anderson
William Belitha	Francis Eyles	Richd: Bundy
Robt: More	Rogers Holland	Edwd: Digby
Ja: Vernon	William Sloper	
Thos: Tower	John Burton	
Geo: Heathcote	George Carpenter	

A true Copy
Ja: Vernon[39]

❧ At a Meeting of the Associates for Mr D'allone's Charity for Converting the Negroes in America, and for other good Purposes at Manwarings's Coffee House on Thursday the twenty sixth Day of November Anno 1730, at nine of the Clock in the Morning Mr Oglethorpe in the Chair, there being present Mr Heathcote, Mr Hughes,

Mr Bundy, Mr Smith, Mr Anderson, Captain Coram and Arthur Bedford.

Two Letters from Mr Fox of Reading, and another from Colonel Johnson Governour of Carolina were read.[40]

1 Agreed, that the Deeds and Publick Writings relating to these Associates be read on the tenth Day of December next, in Order to be entered in the Book bought for that Purpose, and that publick Notice be given thereof accordingly in the printed Summons.

2 The Minute of the last Meeting Num. 21. being taken into Consideration, it is agreed that the Parochial Libraries be sent as soon as possible, and that Mr Smith do make a Report in Writing of the Number of Erasmus his Ecclesiastes, which remain for the Use of these Associates, and that the said Books be sent as soon as possible to the common Store.

3 Agreed, that the Committee for Parochial Libraries, do settle the Number of Libraries of fifteen Pounds Value which can be sent out of the Common Store.

4 Agreed, That a fifth Part of the Number of Erasmus his Ecclesiastes, which shall be sent to Oxford and Cambridge be sent also to the four Universities in Scotland.

5 Agreed, That the Number of Books to be sent of the same to the University of Dublin be considered at some other Meeting.

6 It being proposed, that there be a Dinner, the Charges thereof to be as an Ordinary, after the Allowance made by Dr Bray for this Purpose by his Will, and that the Expences be born by those, who shall be then present, it passed in the Affirmative.

7 It being proposed, that an Abstract of the Minutes of the preceding Year, to be first approved of at a Meeting of these Associates, be then read over to those, who shall be present, it passed in the Affirmative.

8 It being proposed, that the Accounts be audited and settled before the first Day of February, and that on that Day a Treasurer

or Treasurers be chosen for the Year ensuing, it passed in the Affirmative.

9 Agreed, that a Committee be appointed for the Auditing of the said Accounts.

10 A new Impression of Mr Blairs Sermons on the fifth, sixth and seventh Chapters of St Matthew being taken into Consideration, and a Motion being made, that the same be referred to the Committee for Parochial Libraries, it passed in the Affirmative.

Adjourned to Tuesday [sic] December 10th, at nine of the Clock.

[The Board of Trade and Plantations, December 3, 1730]

Mr. Oglethorpe   Sr. John Ganson   Mr. Towers   Mr. Hucks and Mr. Heathcote attending they presented to the Board an Order of the Committee of Council dated the 23rd. of the last Month referring to the Board a Petn. from the Lord Percival and several others praying for a Charter of Incorporation for settling poor people in South Carolina in which Province they desire a Tract of Land may be granted for that purpose And the said order being read their Lordps. desired these Gentlemen would put into Writing their particular proposals upon this subject and bring them to this Office as soon as may be that the Board might take them into Consideration which they promis'd to do accordingly[41]

[Board of Trade and Plantations, December 7, 1730]

Sir   Old Palace Yard Westmr.
                                                  Decr: 7th. 1730

Pursuant to the Orders of the Gentlemen Petitioners to his Majesty for the Establishing of Charitable Colonies in America I send You enclosed their Memorial which they have Drawn up pursuant to the Directions they have received from the Right Honble the Lords of Trade &c

I Desire you would Lay the same before their Lordships and believe me to be

Your most Obedient humble Servt.
James Oglethorpe

To the Right Honoble The Lords Commissioners for Trade & Plantations

In Answer to the Several Questions Your Lordships were pleased to make and in further Explanation of the Subject matter of our Petition we lay before Your Lordships what we think necessary to render our Design (, for relieving such poor Familys as are desirous thereof by Establishing them in America) effectual

First that his Majesty Incorporate the Petitioners by the Name of the Corporation for establishing charitable Colonies in America to have Perpetual succession

To have hold possess enjoy and purchase £1000 p Ann Inheritance in Great Britain and Estates for Lives or Years Goods and Chattels of any Value for the carrying on of the said purposes and to Grant or demise for thirty One Years in Possession only without Fine at the full Rent or with Fine at the Moiety of the full Value

And by that Name to plead and be Impleaded

To have a Common Seal.

To Meet on first of February or Twenty Days after to Chuse proper Officers for the Year ensuing and Elect such Members for the Corporation as they shall think fitt And shall appoint Such further meetings as the said Corporation shall think proper and shall make Such By Laws and Constitutions as shall be thought Necessary and repeal and revoke the same at their Will and pleasure and at any meeting may appoint fit persons to take Subscriptions and Collect money contributed for the purposes aforesaid

To have power of Contracting with and Sending persons into America And to receive and take by Grant Gift purchase and

Otherwise any Lands in America and Cause publick Notification of the said Charter

To Give an Annual Account to the Lord Chancellor the Two Chief Justices the Chief Baron of the Exchequer, the Master of the Rolls for the time being or any Two of them.

Secondly that after the Petitioners are Incorporated his Majesty be Graciously pleased for incouragement of the said Charitable Design unto the said Corporation to Grant the Rivers Savanna and Alatamaha and all the Lands lying between the said Rivers and from the Mouth of the River Savanna all the Coast Southward and as far as the Latitude of 31 Degrees and the Islands Directly opposite to the said Coast to hold of the Manor of East Greenwich in free and common Soccage

And in relation to the regulation of the Intended Settlements We propose to Your Lordships that this Corporation shall have full Power and Authority to Erect Courts of Record or other Courts to be held in the Name of his Majesty for the hearing and Determining of all and all manner of Crimes Offences Pleas processes plaints Actions Matters and things arising between persons Inhabiting or residing within the said Limits whether the said Crimes be Capital or not with Liberty of Appeal to King and Councel where the matter in Dispute shall be above £300.

That the Corporation have a Power of making *Laws Statutes and Ordinances* for the better regulation of and more effectual planting the said Settlements so as the same do not Contradict the Laws of England and be conformable to the Laws of Carolina with regard to the Trade Intercourse and Treaties with the Indians, that the new Settlements be not Subject to the Laws of the Assembly of the said province and that the paper Money shall have no Currency there

That the Corporation shall appoint the Civil Officers necessary for the said regulations who shall take Oaths to his Majesty before they enter upon their Offices

And that the said Civil Officers shall also train and Exercise a Militia and build Towns and fortify in proper Places against the Incursions of the Indians for the Defence of themselves and the Security of South Carolina And that the Governour of South Carolina shall Command the said Militia, the Expence of the said Militia whilst under Armes to be Defrayed by the intended Settlements and be in no manner chargeable to South Carolina

That they have the same Exemption from dutys as were granted to the Province of Carolina by the Charter of King Charles the Second.[42]

[*Board of Trade and Plantations, December 9, 1730*]

The Lord Tyrconnel Mr. Oglethorpe Mr. Hutchinson Mr. Hucks Mr. Heathcote, Sir Wm. Chapman,[43] Sr. Joseph Eyles and several other Gentlemen attending with several Merchants trading to South Carolina Mr. Oglethorpe presented to the Board a Memorial from the Gentlemen concerned in the Petition for a Charter of Incorporation for settling Poor People in South Carolina read the 3rd Inst. And their Lordships upon considering the proposals in the said Memorial acquainted them in answer to that part thereof which relates to their desire of having, holding, possessing enjoying & purchasing £1000 p ann Inheritance in Great Britain and Estates for Lives or Years Goods and Chattels of any value &ca.

1st. That the value of Goods and Chattels must be stinted
2nd. That no Rivers must be granted to them in Propriety but that Rivers must be in Common to all the King's Subjects
3rd. That their Laws must be formed at home revis'd by the King and by His Licence sent to this proposed Colony subject always to his Repeal upon their being found inconvenient
4th. That all the Military Officers in the said Colony must have their Commissions from the Governor of South Carolina
5th. That all the Civil Officers in whom the Execution of the

aforementioned Laws is to be lodged must be approved by the Crown

6th. That they must pay the usual Quit Rent paid in that Province after a Term of Years

Mr. Oglethorpe then acquainted the Board that he would take the Opinion of the Gentlemen concerned on the 6 foregoing propositions and wait upon the Board at another opportunity.[44]

॥§ At a Meeting of the Associates for Mr Dallone's Charity for Converting the Negroes in America, and for other good Purposes at Manwaring's Coffee House on Thursday the tenth Day of December 1730, Major Selwyn in the Chair, there being present Mr Smith, Captain Coram Mr Anderson, ⟨Mr Bundy⟩ - - - and Arthur Bedford.

The Report of the Committee of the Associates for Parochial Libraries was read, and is as followeth.

At a Committee of the Associates on Munday the thirtieth Day of December [November], there being present Mr Hales, Mr Bundy, Mr Smith, and Arthur Bedford,

The several Letters referred to the Committee were read, and the Accounts given of the State of the Libraries in each respective Parish, the Gratitude of the Incumbents mentioned in those Letters, their Promises to keep their Libraries safe and in good Condition, and to comply with such Terms as are, or shall be required by the Associates for that Purpose, and particularly the Readiness of the Parish of Burwell in the County of Cambridge in Building a Room for a safe Repository of their Parochial Library gave great Satisfaction to the Committee.

Agreed, that it is the Opinion of this Committee, that the Incumbents of those Parishes, whither Parochial Libraries have been sent, and who have not given the Bonds required by Act of Parliament, be desired to give the same.

Agreed, that it is the Opinion of this Committee, that the Bonds so executed be first transmitted to the Associates. to be by them registred, in the Manner, which they shall think proper, and then sent to the Bishops of each Diocess, as the Act directs.

Agreed, that it is the Opinion of this Committee, that for the Future no Library be delivered, without Requiring that a Bond be immediately given upon the Delivery or Receipt of the same.

Agreed, that it is the Opinion of this Committee, that it be recommended to each Incumbent, who shall receive a Parochial Library, to catechize the Children, and expound upon the Church Catechism, either from the Pulpit or the Desk, as often as shall be consistent with their other Parochial Duties.

Agreed, that it is the Opinion of this Committee, that those Gentlemen, who desire Augmentations to their Libraries be obliged with the Addition of some of those Books in the Store, of which there remains the greatest Number of Copies, and which therefore can best be spared. Referred to the next Meeting.

Agreed, that it is the Opinion of this Committee, that a Library of fifteen Pounds Value be sent to How in the County of Norfolk, according to the Desire of the Lady Betty Hastings, and that in Regard to Her Ladyships frequent Benefactions and great Charity, no Deductions be made for any Expences concerning the said Library.

Agreed, that it is the Opinion of this Committee, that two Libraries of fifteen Pounds each all incidental Charges included, be sent, one of them to Colerne in Wiltshire, and the other to Stretly in Bedford Shire, at the Desire of Mr Fox of Reading.

Agreed, that it is the Opinion of this Committee, that no more Books be sent out of the Store for Founding any fresh Libraries, unless in very extraordinary Cases any faster than the Associates shall be enabled by their Benefactions to defray the Charges of the same.

Agreed, that it is the Opinion of this Committee, that for the Future, all Incumbents receiving Parochial Libraries do pay for the Carriage of the same.

Adjourned to Wednesday December the second, at three of the Clock in the Afternoon.

At a Committee of the Associates for Parochial Libraries on Wednesday December the second, there being present Mr Hales, Mr Bundy, Mr Smith and Arthur Bedford.

Agreed, that it is the Opinion of this Committee, that if a Clause or Clauses relating to the Establishment of Parochial Libraries, viz, such as were referred to them, or others to the like Effect should hereafter be obtained in any Act of Parliament, it would very much promote and Advance that Branch of the Trust of these Associates, which relates to such Libraries.

Agreed, that it is the Opinion of this Committee that if they shall think proper to give the Summe of fifty Pounds for the Privilege of Printing the next Impression of Mr Blair's Discourses on our Saviour's Sermon on the Mount, it will turn to a good Account to these Associates in their Parochial Libraries.

The said Report was agreed to by these Associates.

The Letter from Mr Burton of Corpus Christi College in Oxford dated Dec. 4. was read, and agreed that Mr Smith prepare an Answer to the same, to be communicated to these Associates.

Dr. Bray's Will was read, and it is agreed that the whole be transcribed in one of the Books bought for that Purpose.

Agreed, that the Day for Preaching and the Dinner be either on the 23d or 25th Day of February as shall be determined on some other Meeting, unless they shall fix on some other Day.

Agreed, that Arthur Bedford do prepare a Paper to be added to the End of Erasmus his Ecclesiastes, to be considered at the next Meeting.

Agreed, that it be proposed to the next Meeting of these Associates to appoint a Committee, to read over the remaining Deeds, and report to the Associates what are fit to be inserted into the Book bought for that Purpose, and what are not.

Adjourned to Thursday the fourteenth Day of January next.
Cha: Selwyn[45]

[*Board of Trade and Plantations, December 15, 1730*]

Mr Oglethorpe attending with Mr Heathcote and Mr Hucks their Lordps took again into consideration the Memorial presented by Mr. Oglethorpe in relation to a Charter of Incorporation for settling poor people in South Carolina read the 9th Inst. As also the Propositions made to them at the same time   And Mr Oglethorpe acquainted the Board that having Consulted the several Gentlemen concerned in this affair they had directed him to inform the Board that as to the 1st. relating to the value of their Goods and Chattels should the same be limited to a large sum they apprehended it might be a prejudice to their undertaking   And if to a small sum it might not answer the End proposed and therefore desired they might not be stinted as to Value   In answer to the 2d. Vizt. That no Rivers should be granted to them in propriety he said they submitted thereto but desired their Grant might be bounded Southerly by the most Southern Branch of the River Alatamaha and northerly by the most large and navigable Branch of the Savannah. In answer to the 3rd. relating to the manner of making their Laws they agreed that the Laws to be made by this Corporation should be immediately laid before the King And if not disapproved of by him they might be sent over and be in full force until the King shall think fit to disallow them   In answer to the 4th and 5th they agreed that all their Judges Justices of the peace and all their Commissioned Military Officers should be approved by the King. In answer to the 6th they agreed to pay the Province Quit Rents for their Lands as the same should be improved. Their Lordps then agreed to consider further of this Affair tomorrow morning.[46]

[*Board of Trade and Plantations, December 16, 1730*]

Their Lordships taking again into consideration the Order of the Committee of Council referring to the Board a Petition from the Lord Percival and several others praying for a Charter of Incorporation for settling Poor People in South Carolina and the Memorial from Mr. Oglethorpe mentioned in the Minutes of the 3rd. and 9th. Instant gave directions for preparing the Draft of a Report thereupon [47]

[*Board of Trade and Plantations, December 17, 1730*]

To the Right Honble the Lords of the Committee of His Majesty's Most Honble Privy Council.

My Lords,

Your Lordships having been pleas'd to refer to Us, the Petition of the Rt. Honble: the Lord Viscount Percival, the Honble: Edwd. Digby, the Honble: Geo: Carpenter, James Oglethorpe Esqrs, and several others, whose Names are thereto subscribed setting forth, That the Cities of London & Westminster, and Parts Adjacent do abound with great Numbers of Indigent persons, who are reduced to such Necessity as to become Burthensome to the Publick, and who would be willing to seek a Lively hood in any of His Majtys: Plantations in America if they were provided with a Passage, & Means of settling there: And humbly proposing to undertake the Trouble & Charge of Transporting all such poor persons and Families, Provided they may obtain a Grant of Lands, in South Carolina, for that Purpose, together with such Powers as shall enable them to Contract with Persons inclinable to settle there, and to receive the Charitable Contributions & Benefactions of all such Persons as are willing to Encourage so good a Design; We have consider'd the several Particulars therein contain'd, And having Discoursed with the Petitioners thereupon, We have receiv'd certain Proposals from them relating to the Subject Matter of their

Petition, whereupon We take Leave to Represent to Your Lordships.

That as the Petitioners Design appears to Us, to be a very laudable One, in every Respect, and may if happily Executed produce many good Effects to the Publick, We think it may deserve due Encouragement, and are humbly of Opinion, that it may be proper for His Majesty to Grant them all reasonable Powers, for the promoting and carrying on so good a Work and therefore We would propose to your Lordships.

That His Majesty may be graciously pleased to Incorporate the Petitioners according to the Prayer of their Petition as a Charitable Society by the Name of The Corporation for establishing charitable Colonies in America, with perpetual Succession

That they may be impowered to purchase Lands of Inheritance in Great Britain, to the value of £1,000 p Annum & Estates for Lives or Years, and Goods and Chattels to any Value; And to receive and take by Grant, Gift, Purchase, or other wise any Lands in America, with Power to make reasonable By Laws, not repugnant to the Laws of Great Britain for the Government of their Corporation; Together with all other Clauses usual and necessary for such a Corporation; And to give an Annual Account of all Monies or Effects by them received or Expended for the carrying on this Charity in the High Court of Chancery.

And as a further Encouragement to this Design, We are of Opinion, His Majesty may be graciously pleased to Grant to the Petitioners & to their Successors for ever all that Tract of Land in His Province of South Carolina lying between the Rivers Savanah & Alatamaha to be Bounded by the most Navigable and largest Branches of the Savanah & the most Southerly Branch of the Alatamaha, with the Islands in the Sea, lying opposite to the said Land, reserving to His Majesty, His Heirs and Successors a Quit Rent, at the Rate of four shillings Proclamation Mony for every Hundred Acres, containd in the said Tract, which shall be Leased or Granted out by the Corporation to their under Tenants, or taken up, Settled or improved by them, or their Agents, the said Quit Rent not to commence or be paid, till Ten years after such Leases, Settlements takings up or Improvements respectively.

And that His Majesty may always be duly informd of what Quantities of Land are Granted, Taken up, Settled or Improved by the sd Corporation, That a constant Register shall be kept by their Officers, of all such Leases, Grants, Takings up, Settlements & Improvements; And Authentick Transcripts thereof annually transmitted to his Majesty's Auditor of the Plantations, or his Deputy, in South Carolina and also to His Majestys Land Surveyor in that Province, reserving to the said Surveyor, in His Majestys behalf, a Right of Inspecting the Lands so Leased, Granted, Taken up, Improved or Settled, to prevent any Abuses with respect to the Quit Rents hereby intended to be reserved upon such Lands.

And whereas, it is the Desire of the Petitioners, that the Tract of Land by them petitioned for, which is at present intirely Uninhabited, except by some few Indian Families, may be seperated from the Province of South Carolina, and be made a Colony, independent thereof, with respect to their Laws, Government and Oeconomy, both Civil and Military, save only in the Command of their Militia which is to remain with His Majestys Governor of South Carolina for the Time being, We are humbly of Opinion that His Majty. may be graciously pleased to indulge them in this particular likewise, saving always the Dominion of the Crown & the Dependance which every British Colony ought to have upon His Majesty. And for this purpose We would humbly propose, that the Corporation may have the Liberty from time to time, to lay before His Majesty, Lists of all such Officers both Civil and Military, as shall be thought necessary by them for the Support, Conduct and Government of their intended Colony, & which are usually appointed by Commissions from His Majesty, or from his Majestys Governors in other Colonies in America; & that when his Majesty shall have approved of such Officer by his Order in Council the Corporation may be impowered to give them Commissions under their common Seal.

And as it will be necessary that there should be Power of making Laws for the Government of this Colony, We would propose that His Majesty may Impower the Corporation from time to time to prepare Laws for that purpose, to be laid before the King in Council, and if not Disapprov'd by his Majesty in 30 Days, that they may be sent over & be in full Force until the King shall think fit to signify his Disallowance of them.

And as in process of time it is to be hoped this Colony may prove a flourishing Settlement and thereby become Sharers in the Trade of South Carolina, it will be necessary that the Person who superintends this Settlemt:, altho he should not Act under the Title of Governor should according to the Act of the 7th & 8th of King William, not only be approved of by His Majesty, as has been before proposed, but also take the usual Oath to Observe the Acts of Trade and Navigation; For which purpose it will be necessary that the usual Instructions upon that Head, which are given to the Governors in America, should likewise be given to him; And that the Corporation do give constant Accounts of all Proceedings to this Office that We may lay the same before His Majesty. We are,

My Lords, Your Lordships, Most Obedient and most humble Servants,

Whitehall
Decemr. 17th. 1730

Westmoreland
P. Docminique.
T. Pelham.
M. Bladen
A: Croft.[48]

[*Privy Council, January 12, 1731*]

By a Committee of the Lords of His Majestys most Honoble Privy Councill.

The Lords of the Committee having this day taken into their Consideration, a Report made by the Lords Commissioners for Trade and Plantations, upon the Petition of the Right Honourable the Lord Viscount Percival, the Honourable Edward Digby, the Honourable George Carpenter, James Oglethorpe Esqrs: and severall others, whose names are thereunto Subscribed, relating to the Establishing a Charitable Colony in South Carolina—And their Lordships having been Attended by the Petitioners, who proposed the making some Alterations in the said Report. Their Lordships are thereupon pleased to Order, as it is hereby Ordered that the annexed Paragraph of the said Report, Be Referred back to the said Lords Commissioners, together with the Alteration proposed by the Petitioners to be made thereto; And the said Lords Commissioners are to hear the Petitioners thereupon, and Report their Opinion to this Committee, whether any Alteration is proper to be made in the said Paragraph, and in case They are of Opinion that any Alteration should be made therein, to Report the same to their Lordships.

           Temple Stanyan

And whereas it is the desire of the Petitioners, that the Tract of Land by them petitioned for, which is at present entirely uninhabited, except by some few Indian Familys, may be separated from the Province of South Carolina, and be made a Colony independant thereof with respect to their Laws, Government and Oeconomy, both Civil and Military, save only in the Command of their Militia, which is to remain with His Majestys Governor of South Carolina for the time being: We are humbly of Opinion that His Majesty may be Graciously pleased to indulge them in this particular likewise Saving always the Dominion of the Crown and the Dependance which every British Colony ought to have upon His Majesty; And for this Purpose we would humbly Propose; that the Corporation may have the Liberty from time to time *to lay before His Majesty Lists of all such Officers both Civil and Mili-*

tary as shall be thought necessary by them for the Support, Conduct and Government of their intended Colony, and which are ususally appointed by Commissions from His Majesty or from His Majesty's Governors in other Colonys in America; And that when His Majesty shall have approved of such Officers by His Order in Councill, the Corporation may be impowered to give them Commissions under their Common Seal.

The Alteration proposed to be made to the aforegoing Paragraph by the Petrs: in lieu of the Lines under Scored.

Under their Common Seal to constitute Courts of Record and other Courts to be held in His Majestys Name, and for the Space of twenty one Years to appoint and displace all Officers Civil and Military within the said District together with such other Powers as have been granted on the first Establishment of Colonys.⁴⁹

[*Board of Trade and Plantations, January 13, 1731*]

An order of the Committee of Council dated the 12th Inst referring back to this Board a paragraph in their Report, which the Petitioners for settling poor people in Carolina propose to be altered, was read. And the Board gave directions that Mr. Oglethorpe & the Gentlemen concerned in the Petition should be desired to attend the Board tomorrow morning.⁵⁰

[*Board of Trade and Plantations, January 14, 1731*]

Mr. Oglethorpe, Mr. Hucks   Mr. Heathcote   Mr. Coram and sevl. other Gentlemen attending as they had been desired their Lordships took again into Consideratn. the Order of the Committee of Council relating to the settling poor people in South Carolina read yesterday. And after some discourse with these Gentlemen thereupon a Report to the Lords of the Committee was agreed and signed.⁵¹

To The Rt: Honbl: the Lords of the Committee &c

My Lords.

Your Lordps: having been pleas'd by Your Order of the 12: Inst: to refer back to us a Par: of our Rept: upon the Petn. of the Rt: Honble: the Ld: Visct: Percival, the Honble: Edd: Digby, the Honble: Geo: Carpenter, James Oglethorpe Esqrs: And sevl: others relating to the establishing a charitable Colony in South Carolina; together with an Alteration propos'd by the Petrs: to be made to our said Report   We have consider'd the same And having discours'd with them thereupon, We take leave to acquaint your Lordps:

That We do not apprehend any great Inconvenience that can arise to the Publick if his M.Jy: should be graciously pleas'd to allow the Petrs: *under their common Seal to constitute Courts of Record And other Courts, to be held in his Mys Name, And for the Space of Twenty One Years to appoint and displace all Officers Civil & Military within the said District,* But the last Words in the Alterats: propos'd by them being too general vizt, *together with such other Powers as have been granted on the first Establishment of Colonies;* We propose to add in the stead thereof the following Words. *together with such other Powers as may be necessary for the Support And Defence of the said Colony.*

  We are &c.   P Docminique
          T Pelham
  Whitehall   M Bladen
  Januy 14: 1730/1 O Bridgeman
          Ja Brudenell.[52]

 At a Meeting of the Associates for Mr Dallones Charity for Converting the Negroes in America, and for other good Purposes at Manwarings Coffee House on Thursday the fourteenth Day of January 1730/1   Mr Oglethorpe in the Chair, there being also present Mr Hughes, Mr Burton, Captain Coram, Mr Anderson, Mr Smith and Arthur Bedford.

A Letter from Dr [Richard] Baldwyn Provost of Dublin College in Ireland, concerning Erasmus his Ecclesiastes was read.

Mr Newman's Letter concerning the Printing 100 of Dr Brays Books left by his Will to begin a Parochial Library in any Market Town to be sold for 5oli was read.

Arthur Bedford also acquainted the Associates, that the Society for Promoting Christian Knowledge had given four and twenty Treatises against Perjury, and Subornation of Perjury,[53] to be put in Parochial Libraries.

Agreed, that the Thanks of these Associates be given to the said Society for their Kindness in both the above mentioned Particulars.

Arthur Bedford reported, that he had examined the Books in The Store Room, to see, if any other Libraries can be made out for other Benefactors, after those to How, Stretly and Collerne are sent away, and according to the best Account of further Libraries, the Value of them are as followeth.

	li.	s	d		li	s.	d
Libr. 1.	10.	00.	00	Libr. 7.	5.	00.	02
Libr. 2	9.	05.	04	Libr. 8	4.	17.	08
Libr. 3	6.	06.	04	Libr. 9	4.	13.	09
Libr. 4	6.	05.	01	Libr. 10	4.	09.	09
Libr. 5	6.	00.	07	Libr. 11	4.	09.	09
Libr. 6	6.	00.	06	Libr. 12	4.	09.	09

The Report of the Committee, to whom the Affairs of Parochial Libraries were referred, concerning Books to be sent to the Libraries already endowed, being taken into Consideration, (it is agreed, that one be bound to How in Norfolk Shire, and that those of Stretly and Collerne be adjourned til the Accounts are audited) was received.

The Report of the same Committee concerning the Printing of some of Mr Blairs Discourses on our Saviours Sermon on the Mount being taken into Consideration, it is agreed that it be farther deferred, and since reported not to be advantageous

Arthur Bedford reported, that some well disposed Gentlemen seem'd inclinable to give a Summe of Mony for the Purchasing of Edwards his Body of Divinity in Quires,[54] being three Volumes in Folio, to send to all the Libraries already founded by Dr Bray, upon Condition, that these Associates did pay for the Binding of them; but that at present they might bind them out of the same Mony, and only lay out the same Summe for the Purchase of more of the same Books, when they should be in a Condition for that Purpose, it is agreed that the Associates will thankfully accept of the said Proposal.

Arthur Bedford reported, that he was informed by Mr Martin,[55] that he had about 1100 of Erasmus his Ecclesiastes in his Custody, and that he thinks Dr Bray had disposed of about 100 more, and that he insisted on 2s. 9d for the Price of them in Quires; But Martin appearing this Day he offered the whole at 2s. 6d, which is referred to the Consideration of the next Meeting.

⟨Agreed that the Consideration of Reprinting Mr Blairs Discourses on our Saviour's Sermon on the Mount, be referred to the next Meeting⟩

⟨Agreed, that Mr Martin be at Liberty to sell the Erasmus his Ecclesiastes, which do not belong to these Associates, as he shall think best for his own Advantage, and that they will take off Such as belong to them at 2s. 9d each.⟩

Arthur Bedford according to Order delivered to these Associates a Catalogue of the Books, which Dr Bray left by Will to be disposed of for 50li to begin a Library in any Market Town of Great Britain, and the same was ordered to be kept by Mr Anderson, and another by the said Arthur Bedford.

Agreed, that the Sermon to be preached concerning the Instruction of the Negroes in the Christian Religion, be preached on Tuesday the 23d. Day of February, at 11 of the Clock, ⟨at⟩ in the Parish Church of St Austins near St Pauls if the Use of the said Church can be had, and that Mr Samuel Smith be desired to preach the same.

A Motion being made that after Sermon there be a Dinner, and the Charges thereof to be as an Ordinary, to be born by those, who shall be then present, except 40s given by Dr Bray for that Purpose, it passed in the Affirmative

Agreed, that the Place be at the Kings Arms in St Pauls Church Yard. and that Mr Oglethorpe be the Steward for that Purpose.

A Motion being made, that an Abstract of the Minutes for the preceding Year to be first approved of at a Meeting of these Associates be then read over to those, who shall be present, it passed in the Affirmative to be drawn up by Arthur Bedford.

⟨Agreed that - - - be the Treasurer for the Year ensuing,⟩

Agreed that a Committee be appointed on that Day for the for the [sic] Auditing of the Accounts for the Year past

Arthur Bedford according to Order laid before the Associates, an Appendix to be added to Erasmus his Ecclesiastes, which was perused at the same Time by four several Members, and a Motion being made that the same be printed, ⟨accordingly, it passed in the - - - ⟩ it is agreed, that that Part be printed which gives Hope of Printing the other Parts.

Agreed, that a Day be appointed to read over the remaining Deeds, and report to the Associates, what are fit to be inserted in the Book ⟨of Letters⟩, bought for that Purpose, and what are not.

A Proposal being made, that 7 Books of Erasmus his Ecclesiastes be sent to Dr Baldwyn to Dublin College in Ireland, it - - -

A Motion being made, that the Books designed for the Libraries which are designed for How, Stretly and Collerne, which are in Quires be bound, in Order to send away the said Libraries, it passed in the - - -

Agreed, that the Lord Percivall. Col. Carpenter, Mr Vernon,

Mr Heathcote, Mr Hucks, Mr Towers, Mr Eyles, Mr La Roche, and Mr Oglethorpe, and Mr Moore be a Committee for Solliciting the Grant for the Lands designed for the Charitable Colony in South Carolina in America.[56]

Mr Martin paid 2li. 8s. 8d, and bills allowed him in the whole 6li. 0s, 0d.

Mr Burton paid 5li. 5s, to the Associates the gift of Mr Randolph of Corpus Christi College,[57] to their religious Designs in General,

Agreed, that the Thanks of the Associates be given to the Benefactor

Mr Burton presented the Associates with two Latin Sermons of his own Making, with the Right of Copy,[58] and their thanks were returned to him accordingly.

Mr Burton recommended the Vicarage of Buckland in the County of Berks for a Parochial Library of 10li Value, which was referred to the Consideration of the next Meeting, referred further.

Adjourned to Thursday the 28th Day of this Instant January.

At a Meeting of the Associates for Mr Dallone's Charity for Converting the Negroes in America and for other good Purposes at Manwarings Coffee House on Thursday the twenty eighth Day of January 1730 Mr Oglethorpe in the Chair, there being present Mr Digby, Captain Coram, Mr Anderson, Mr Eyles, Mr Vernon, Major Selwyn

The Particulars of the 14th Instant, which through extraordinary Business were omitted in the last Meeting were taken into Consideration and agreed to, as before mentioned.

⟨Mr Oglethorpe reported, from the Committee to whom the Obtaining a Charter for a charitable Colony was referred, that - - - ⟩

Agreed that 500 Tickets be printed in These Words.

On Tuesday Febr. 23 there will be preached a Sermon before the

Associates of Dr Bray deceased at the Parish Church of St Austins near St Pauls Church Prayers to begin at 11 of the Clock. and that they be sent to these Associates.

⟨Agreed that Mr Oglethorpe return the thanks of these Associates, and accept of the same himself, for their good Offices in this Affair, and that they be desired to finish the same with all Expedition⟩

⟨It being reported, that the Fund in which Mr Dallone's Charity is at present placed will sink at our Lady Day next to three Pounds per Cent. Interest, - - - ⟩

Agreed, that Mr Smith and Arthur Bedford draw up a Proposal for further Converting the Negroes in America to be laid before these Associates.

Agreed, that these Associates at their next Meeting do consider of all Proposals and Methods relating to the Instruction and Baptizing the Negroes in America.

Adjourned to Thursday Feb. 11th.

[*Privy Council, January 28, 1731*]

Upon reading this Day at the Board a Report from the Lords of the Committee of His Majestys Most Honourable Privy Councill dated the 18th: of this Instant in the words following Viz.

"Your Majesty having been pleased to referr unto this Committee, the humble Petition of the Right Honourable the Lord Viscount Percival, The Honourable Edward Digby, the Honourable George Carpenter, James Oglethorpe Esqr. and severall others whose Names are thereunto Subscribed, Setting forth, 'That the Citys of London and Westminster and Parts Adjacent, do abound with great Numbers of Indigent Persons, who are reduced to such necessitys, as to become burthensome to the Publick, and who would be willing to Seek a Livelyhood in any of Your Majesty's Plantations in

America, if they were Provided with a Passage and means of Settling there; And humbly proposing to Undertake the trouble and Charge of transporting all such poor persons and Familys, provided they may obtain a Grant of Lands in South Carolina for that purpose, together with such Powers, as shall Enable them to receive the Charitable Contributions and Benefactions of all such Persons as are willing to encourage so good a Design—' The Lords of the Committee did, on the twenty third of November last take the said Petition into Consideration, And thought proper to referr the same to the Lords Commissioners for Trade and Plantations—Who having received from the Petitioners certain proposalls relating to the Subject matter of the said Petition, and discoursed with them thereupon, have reported to this Committee, that the design appears to be very laudable in every respect and to deserve due encouragement, and may if happily Executed produce many good Effects to the Publick—And do therefore propose that Your Majesty would be graciously pleased to Incorporate the Petitioners according to the Prayer of their Petition as a Charitable Society by the Name of The Corporation for Establishing Charitable Colonys in America, with Perpetuall Succession, and to Grant them all such reasonable Powers as may be necessary for promoting and carrying on the said Undertaking, The most materiall of which powers, are particularly mentioned in the said Report of the Lords Commissioners for Trade and Plantations:—The Lords of the Committee having taken the said Report into their Consideration, and been Attended by the Petitioners, who proposing severall Alterations to be made therein, particularly with regard to their being Empowered to appoint and Displace all Officers Civil and Military for the term of twenty one Years,—The Committee thought it necessary to receive the further Opinion of the said Lords Commissioners for Trade thereupon Who having considered thereof, have no Objection to Your Majestys granting the Petitioners such a Power: — The Lords of the Committee do therefore Agree humbly to lay before Your Majesty, the severall powers proposed by the said Report of the Lords Commissioners for Trade to be granted to the Petitioners, together with such Alterations as they thought proper to make therein, for Your Majestys Royall Approbation — Vizt:

" 'That the Petitioners may be impowered to purchase Lands of Inheritance in Great Britain to the Value of One thousand Pounds per Annum and Estates for Lives or Years and Goods and Chattels to any Value, and to receive and take by Grant, gift, Purchase or otherwise any Lands in America, with Power to make reasonable By Laws not repugnant to the Laws of Great Britain for the Government of their Corporation, together with all Clauses usuall and necessary for such a Corporation, and to lay an Annuall Account of all Moneys or Effects by them received or expended for the carrying on this Charity before the Lord Chancellor, The Lord Chief Justice of the Kings Bench the Master of the Rolls, the Lord Chief Justice of the Common Pleas the Lord Chief Baron of the Exchequer or any two of them.

" 'That Your Majesty may be graciously pleased to Grant to the Petitioners and to their Successors for ever, all that Tract of Land in Your Province of South Carolina lying between the Rivers Savanah and Alatamaha to be bounded by the most Northern Stream of the Savanah and the most Southerly Stream of the Alatamaha with the Islands in the Sea lying opposite to the said Land; reserving to Your Majesty Your Heirs and Successors a Quit Rent at the rate of four Shillings Proclamation Money for every hundred Acres contained in the said Tract which shall be leased or granted out by the Corporation to their under Tenants, or Settled or improved by them or their Agents, the said Quit Rent not to Commence or be paid till ten Years after such Leases Settlements or Improvements respectively.

" 'That to the end Your Majesty may always be duly informed of what Quantitys of Land are granted Settled or Improved by the said Corporation, that a Constant Register be kept by their Officers, of all such Leases, Grants, Settlements and improvements, and Authentick Transcripts thereof Annually transmitted to Your Majestys Auditor of the Plantations or his Deputy and also to Your Majestys Land Surveyor in South Carolina, reserving to the said Surveyor in Your Majestys behalf, a right of inspecting the Lands so Leased granted improved or Settled to prevent any Abuses with respect to the Quitt Rents intended to be reserved upon such Lands provided that neither the said Auditor, nor his Deputy, nor the said Surveyor, shall take or Demand any Fee or reward from the Corporation or from any Person holding under them, on transmitting the said Accounts, or for Inspecting the said Lands.

" 'That the Tract of Land Petitioned for, which is at present intirely uninhabited except by some few Indian Familys, should be Separated from the Province of South Carolina, and made a Colony Independant thereof, with respect to their Laws, Government and Oeconomy both Civil and Military, save only the Chief Command of their Militia which is to remain with Your Majestys Governor of South Carolina for the time being, and saving always the Dominion of the Crown and the Dependance which every British Colony ought to have upon Your Majesty And for this purpose, that the Corporation should have power under their Common Seal, from time to time to constitute Courts of Record and other Courts to be held in Your Majestys name, And for the Space of twenty one Years to appoint and displace all Officers Civil and Military, except such Officers as shall be constituted and

Appointed for Receiving Collecting and Managing Your Majestys Revenue within the said District; and should likewise have such other powers as may be necessary for the Support and Defence of the said Colony—

" 'That the Corporation should be further impowered from time to time to prepare Laws for the Government of the said Colony to be laid before Your Majesty in Councill, and if such Laws shall not be disapproved by Your Majesty within three Calendar Months after they shall have been so laid before Your Majesty, that they may then be sent over, and be in full force, untill Your Majesty shall think fit to Signify Your disallowance of them—

" 'And lastly, that as in process of time it is to be hoped, this Colony may prove a flourishing Settlement; The said Colony should have liberty given them, to import and export their Goods from any Port that shall be appointed by Your Majesty, without being obliged to touch at any other Port in Carolina.

" 'And tho' this Colony be a New and Seperate District, yet ought it to be Subject to the Act passed in the Seventh and eighth of His late Majesty King William, and to all other Acts now in force in Great Britain relating to Your Majestys Plantations in America in Generall, as if this Colony had been Established before the passing the said Acts; and the Corporation ought also to lay constant Accounts of the progress of the Colony before One of Your Majestys Principall Secretarys of State, and the Lords Commissioners for Trade and Plantations, that Your Majesty may be duly informed thereof.'

"If your Majesty shall be pleased to Approve of what is herein proposed, The Lords of the Committee are humbly of Opinion, That Mr: Attorney and Sollicitor Generall should be directed to prepare a Draught of a Charter agreable to the said Heads."

His Majesty taking the said Report into Consideration, was pleased, with the Advice of His Privy Council, to Approve thereof, and to Order, as it is hereby Ordered, That Mr: Attorney and Mr: Sollicitor Generall, do prepare the Draught of a Charter agreable to what is therein proposed—And that they do insert therein, such Clauses as they shall think proper, to render His Majesty's intentions herein most Effectual—And present the same to His Majesty at this Board, for His Royall Approbation.

A true Copy
Temple Stanyan[59]

[Percival, February 6, 1731]

... in the evening Mr. Oglethorp came again to talk over the Carolina settlement, which is in a good way. The Board of Trade have reported in favour of it, and we the undertakers or managers have the government of the people we send thither for twenty-one years, with a large track of land granted, that lies between two rivers.[60]

[Percival, February 9, 1731]

After dinner I went to the Bedford Arms Tavern in the little peaches Covent Garden, and met Mr. Oglethorp, Colonel Carpenter, Mr. Vernon, Mr. Hucks, Mr Towrs junior, Mr. Heathcote, Captain Heathcote, Mr. Moor, and Mr. Digby, to consider of a scruple arisen in some gentlemen's heads, whether the acceptance of the government of the colony we are sending to Carolina, doth not vacate our seats in Parliament, and what we should do to remedy it, supposing it so. Some gentlemen proposed to take the sense of the House upon it, but others said that was not conclusive, nor of certain security, for we are by our charter to be incorporated for twenty-one years, and another Parliament may be of another mind. Mr. Oglethorp proposed to have a short Act of Parliament to qualify us for holding our seats, as is provided for in the South Sea Act in favour of several members at that time of the House constituted directors of that Company.[61] We all agreed to it, only I proposed Sir Robert Walpole should be first acquainted with it, or otherwise it would look as if we slighted the King's Charter and prerogative, besides that 'tis but a fitting compliment to the Ministry, who if they pleased might from the beginning have stifled our design. So Mr. Oglethorp and I are to acquaint Sir Robert on Thursday next with it, when we meet him in the House.[62]

At a Meeting of the Associates for Mr Dallone's Charity for Converting the Negroes in America, and for other good Purposes, at Manwaring's Coffee House on Thursday the 11th Day of February 1730/1 Mr Vernon in the Chair, there being present Mr Hales, Mr Smith, Mr Anderson, Captain Coram, Mr Belitha and Arthur Bedford[63]

An Abstract of the Proceedings of these Associates, to be read at their Anniversary Feast was read and agreed to with several Amendments.

Agreed, that one of Erasmus his Ecclesiastes be sent to all the Irish Bishops, and that the Lord Percival be spoke with, to know his Opinion, in what Manner they may be best transmitted thither.

A Motion being made that six of Erasmus his Ecclesiastes be sent to Mr Dobbs a fellow of Dublin College,[64] it passed in the affirmative.

Mr Joseph Bonner offering himself to go as a Clergy Man to South Carolina, was informed, that these Associates could not treat with him, without a particular Testimonial from the University of Edinburgh.[65]

Mr Anderson acquainting these Associates that the Earl Thanet had left 40000li to be given to pious and charitable Uses not exceeding 1000li to each, agreed that Application be made for the same for the Use of the Associates.

Mr Hales his Letter to Mr Oglethorpe concerning a Gift of 50li worth in Books for the Conversion of the Negroes was read, Agreed that the Associates do thankfully accept thereof and that Mr Hales returns his Thanks for the same.

Agreed, that Mr Smith do draw up a Catalogue against the next Meeting of such Books, as are proper for this Purpose.

Mr Smith reported, that he had perused the two Books referred to him, which he thinks may be useful, with some Alterations as to Matters of Fact.

Agreed, that Mr Smith be desired to make the said Alterations, by this Day Month.

The said Books were referred to Mr Hales, and he is to report his Opinion thereof on Tuesday sevennight.

To which Time the Associates are adjourned, to meet at the Parish Church of St. Augustines.

Stephen Hales

☙ At a Meeting of the Associates for Mr D'allone's Charity at the Kings Arms near St Pauls on Tuesday the twenty third Day of February 1730/1, there being present Mr Oglethorpe, Mr Hucks, Mr La Roche, Mr Vernon, Mr Belitha, Mr Anderson, Captain Coram, Mr Hales, Mr Smith, Mr Bundy, Mr Burton, Mr Somerschald and Arthur Bedford.

The Thanks of these Associates were unanimously returned to the Reverend Mr Samuel Smith for his excellent Sermon preached before them on this Day, and he was desired to give them Leave to print the same; and it is agreed, that an Account of the Life of Dr Bray the Founder of these Associates be added thereto.

Agreed, that the Reverend Mr Bundy be desired to wait upon the Lord Bishop of London, and that he humbly desires of his Lordship an Account of the Number of the Clergy and Negroes in the several Islands and Plantations in America, with such other Particulars, as his Lordship shall judge proper to promote their Designs in Instructing, Converting and Baptizing the said Negroes.[66]

Adjourned until Thursday the eleventh Day of March next, to Manwaring's Coffee House.

[*Percival, March 5, 1731*]

After this I went to Mr. Oglethorp, who showed me a draft of the charter we are to obtain of the King of the lands in South Carolina wherein to settle a colony, all which I approved; we appointed to-morrow morning for he and I, Lord Tyrconnel and Mr. Heathcot to wait on Lord Carteret upon this affair,[67] whose consent is necessary to the charter, he being a proprietor in the Province of Carolina.[68]

[*Percival, March 6, 1731*]

This day I was called on by Mr. Oglethorp to go to Lord Carteret's to discourse over the Carolina Settlement, he being the only proprietor who has not sold his rights to the Province. His Lordship was not at home, and we agreed to go again Monday morning.[69]

[*Percival, March 8, 1731*]

I waited on Lord Carteret, with Mr. Oglethorp, Hucks, La Roch, and Heathcot, members of Parliament and trustees of the intended Carolina Colony, to acquaint his Lordship with the progress we have made therein, and to ask his Lordship's concurrence and favour, he being still a proprietor of that Province, and his Lordship said he would do what the King should do, securing his right to a seventh part of the lands and quitrent, which the Attorney General is to take care of.[70]

[*Percival, March 9, 1731*]

Mr. Oglethorp and I, with others, spoke to Sir Robert Walpole that it would be necessary to have an Act of Parliament to enable the Crown to grant us a necessary charter for the charitable colony we design to plant in South Carolina, and we desired the Crown would favour it; he said he was not against it, and that I would give him at his house to-morrow heads of a Bill for that purpose.[71]

[*Percival, March 10, 1731*]

This morning I waited on Sir Robert Walpole with the heads of our Bill, to which Sir Robert made so many objections that I found it fruitless to expect we should have leave to bring in a Bill at all, though I urged several good reasons, but I found he was not willing the Colonies should depend on Parliament for their settlement, but merely on the Crown. He objected that the King's prerogative would be subjected thereby to Parliament, that there was no need of a naturalization of those who went thither, that our apprehensions of endangering our seats in Parliament by accepting the trust was an idle fear.

I returned to Mr. Oglethorp with this account.[72]

[*Percival, March 11, 1731*]

To-day I visited cousin Ned Southwell to get him to speak to my late Lord Thanet's trustees of his charitable legacy, that they would give ten thousand pounds thereof to the Carolina settlement. He told me he had spoke already for a thousand pounds to be given to the Incurables of Bedlam Hospital, and as much to the

Westminster Infirmary,⁷³ and as neither of those requests were yet answered, he could not decently speak for a third; but he advised me to speak to Will. Wogan, who is very great with Mr. Cook, brother to the late Vice-Chamberlain Cook, who is one of the trustees of my Lord's charity, and that I must myself find another to speak to Mr. Lamb, who is the other.⁷⁴

§ At a Meeting of the Associates for Mr D'allone's Charity at Manwaring's Coffee House, on Thursday the eleventh Day of March 1730/1, The Reverend Mr Hales in the Chair, there being also present Captain Coram, Mr Anderson, Mr Smith and Arthur Bedford.

The Proceedings of the Associates at their Meetings on the twenty eighth Day of January, and the eleventh and twenty third Days of February were read.

The Proposal of Mr Smith and Arthur Bedford for the further Converting of the Negroes in America was read.

Agreed, that the same be kept with the Letters, to be perused when Occasion shall require.

Agreed, that such Amendments be made thereto in Order to be printed whenever the Associates shall think, it may be serviceable to their Designs.

The Lord Percival having been consulted concerning the Sending of an Erasmus his Ecclesiastes to each of the Irish Bishops, answered, that he would readily undertake it, and that the Number of the Irish Bishops were two and twenty. His Lordship also delivered up a Note of five Pounds upon Mr D'allone's Trustees to be cancelled, which was cancelled accordingly. Agreed, that the Thanks of these Associates be returned to his Lordship for his Favours to these Associates in both Particulars.

The Catalogue drawn up by Mr Smith of such Books, which might be useful to be sent to the Missionaries in America.

Agreed, that the Sending of them into America be reconsidered at some other Meeting.

Mr Hales reported concerning the Treatises referred to him relating to Parochial Libraries, and the Conversion of the Negroes, in Order to be printed, that he is of the same Opinion with Mr Smith, which he reported on the 11th Day of February.

Agreed, that the said Treatises be referred to Mr Bundy, and that he reports his Opinion thereof on this Day Fortnight.

Mr Smith reported, that the Sermon which he preached on the twenty third Day of February, was perused by Mr Burton in Order to be printed, which Sermon was now referred to Mr Hales and Arthur Bedford, and it is agreed, that after their Perusal thereof, it be immediately sent to the Press, and that a thousand of them be printed.[75]

The Accounts of Arthur Bedford for the Year past was audited, and agreed, that they be signed by the Chairman, and the Ballance due to him was six Pounds, three Shillings and ten Pence halfpeny.

Agreed, that Mr Smith do bring in his Accounts on this Day fortnight.

A Proposal being made, that a Library of ten Pounds Value be sent to the Parish of Buckland in the County of Berks, at the Request of Mr Burton, it passed in the Affirmative.

Arthur Bedford reported, that he had waited on an intended Benefactor, for the Conversion of the Negroes in America, who proposed a Parliamentary Method for the Sending over more learned and faithful Clergy for that Purpose, to which he should be willing to be a Contributor.

Agreed, that the Thanks of these Associates be returned to the said Benefactor for Communicating his Scheme to them, but the Members of the House of Commons being engaged to attend in Parliament, it is ordered to be reconsidered at a full Meeting, when they are present.

Mr Thomas Page, a Stationer on Tower Hill having promised an hundred Pounds for the charitable Colony,[76] agreed that these

Associates return him their Thanks for the same, and that they deal with him in his said Trade, as Occasion shall require.

The Reverend Mr Somerschald sent four Pounds and four Shillings by the Reverend Mr Smith, for the Designs of Parochial Libraries, and it is agreed, that the Thanks of the Associates be returned to him for his Benefaction.

Mr Somerschald also desired, that when the Affairs of this Society will permit, they would send a Library to Dover in Kent, which was agreed to accordingly.

Five Guineas were also sent by Mr ⟨Hales⟩ Smith from an unknown Benefactor for Parochial Libraries, and it is agreed that the Thanks of the Associates be returned to the said Benefactor.

Five Guineas more were also sent by the said Mr ⟨Hales⟩ Smith for Preaching in the Prisons, or otherwise for parochial Libraries, and it is agreed, that the Thanks of the Associates be also returned to the said Benefactor.

Michael Terry on Ludgate Hill, and Sebastian Trotman of the Parish of St Martins le Grand offering themselves to go to the charitable Colony, were desired to attend on this Day fortnight, when it is supposed, that some of the Members of Parliament will be present.

Mr Anderson reported, that he had spoken with Mr James Martin concerning Erasmus his Ecclesiastes, who was willing to afford the whole Number, being 1200 to the Associates for two Shillings and three Pence each in Quires.

Agreed, that the same be reconsidered at some other Meeting.

Adjourned to Thursday March the twenty fifth.

Steph: Hales

[*Percival, March 19, 1731*]

To-day Mr. Oglethorp called on me, that we might speak to Sir Robert Walpole for lottery tickets for the advantage of the Georgia Colony. I promised to meet him at the House. . . .

Afterwards I went to the House, where I spoke to Sir Robert Walpole, who promised to set down the names of subscribers thereto as far as two thousand tickets, but said the lottery was already so much more than full, that there must be a striking off.[77] However, that he would strike us off but in proportion with others. I told him it was a kind promise, that this was meaned by us for a foundation to carry on our intended colony, and if we could get two thousand tickets, it would be one thousand pounds in our pockets for the colony; having engaged citizens who would give us a premium on the tickets of ten shillings each.[78]

[*Percival, March 22, 1731*]

. . . at six went to Mr. Heathcot's in Soho Square, where several gentlemen of the Carolina Colony met, and afterwards waited on the Attorney General in Lincoln's Inn, to give him the Order of Council relating to our affairs, and to acquaint him that Mr. Towers, one of our members, would bring him our thoughts on the charter desired.[79]

At a Meeting of the Associates for Mr D'allones Charity at Manwarings Coffee House on Thursday the 25th Day of March 1731, Mr Oglethorpe in the Chair, there being also present Mr Hales, Mr Anderson, Mr Smith and Arthur Bedford.

A Letter from the Minister of How in the County of Norfolk, and another from Mr Somerschald concerning Parochial Libraries were read.

Agreed to pay the Ballance of the Account to this Day being 6li. 7s. 1½d to Arthur Bedford, and the said was paid accordingly by Mr Oglethorpe.

Mr Smith was again desired to bring in his Accounts by this Day fortnight.

	li.	s.	d
Paid to Mr Oglethorpe by Smith, on Account of Two benefactors unknown—for Parochial Libraries	5.	5.	0
For Preaching in the Prisons, or for Want thereof as Ditto	5.	5.	0
From Mr Somerschald for Parochial Libraries	4.	4.	0

Agreed that 600 of Erasmus his Ecclesiastes be bound in Calf, at 9d each 100 being bound for the payment for 96, that one half be bound by Mr Page and the other by Mr Cholmondeley.

Stephen Lee with his Wife three Sons and a Daughter offered themselves to go to the charitable Colony, living in Lemon Street in Goodman's Fields.

Adjourned to Thursday the eighth Day of April next.

[*Percival, March 29, 1731*]

... I gave Sir Robert Walpole the names of twenty persons who we of the Carolina Company desired tickets in the intended lottery for each one hundred tickets. He took the paper, and said he would take care of it.[80]

[*Percival, April 7, 1731*]

I then went to see Mr. Wogan, to desire he would speak to Mr. Cook, brother to the late Vice-Chamberlain, who with Mr. Lamb, a lawyer,[81] was left disposer of the late Earl of Thanet's charity, amounting to the sum of forty-thousand pounds, to be given as they approved in forty different charities of one thousand pounds each. I desired he would inform Mr. Cook of the King's grant of lands in Carolina to me and others for planting a colony there, and that we hoped he would think a thousand pounds of that charity well disposed in helping to raise a fund for supporting the people sent. He said he would speak.[82]

At a Meeting of the Associates for Mr D'allone's Charity at Manwarings Coffee House on Thursday the eighth Day April 1731, Mr Digby in the Chair, there being also present Mr Vernon, Captain Coram, and Arthur Bedford. Mr Hales

A Letter from Mr John Copping was read, Apothecary Chiryregon [Chirurgeon] and Schoolmaster offering himself to go to Carolina, together with a Neighbour of his, who is a Shoemaker.

A Motion being made, that every one, who goes to the Colony give a Bond to settle in no other Place, referred ad Deliberandum.

Agreed, that Mr Smith's Sermon be referred to Mr Anderson

An Account of the Particular Expenses, which will be necessary for the Carrying on of the Designs of the Associates of Dr Bray with Success, were read before them, and agreed to be entered in the Minutes, and are as followeth.

To defray the Charges of the whole last Year, as p Account.

To defray the Expences of the Decree in Chancery relating to the Negroes.

To defray the Expences of the Charter for the Colony.

To print the anniversary Sermon.

To print some Account of the Life of Dr Bray.

To print a Treatise to encourage Benefactions for the charitable Colony.

To print a Treatise to promote the Conversion and Baptizing of the Negroes.

To print a Treatise to encourage Parochial Libraries.

To print in Folio Rules for Preserving Parochial Libraries.

To print Proposals for a Method of Instructing the Blacks.

To print an annual Account of the Proceedings of the Associates, beginning at the End of the next Year.

To bind up Register Books for Parochial Libraries.

To bind up all the Books in the Store Room, which are to be sent to parochial Libraries.

To bind up the Books, which are in Mr Cholmondeley's Hands.

To bind up all the Books in the Store Room, which are to be sent to the Missionaries in America.

To bind up as many of Erasmus his Ecclesiastes, as are necessary to be sent to the Universities, Bishops, Plantations, and Parochial Libraries.

To buy the Rest of the same, which are in Mr Martin's Hands.

To bind them up when bought.

To stich Books to be sent to the Parishioners with Parochial Libraries.

To buy practical Sermons in 4to for 1d each, which will bind up with the half Sheets in the Store house.

To bind up the Treatises of Dr Clarke for parochial Libraries.

To buy Edwards his Body of Divinity, as many as can be had in Quires.

To bind them up, if they can any Way be had.

To defray the Charges of Transcribing the Accounts, Minutes, Letters, Deeds &c into the Books bought for that Purpose.

To defray the Charges of the ensuing Year,

And to set others a good Example.

A Motion being made, that the Gift of Mr Randolf of Corpus Christi College in Oxford, being five Pounds, be applied for the Binding up of Erasmus his Ecclesiastes for the Use of the University of Oxford it passed in the Affirmative.

A Motion being made, that the Mony arising from the Books sold out of the Store Room for America in Pursuance of the Gift of fifty Pounds for that Purpose be applied for the more speedy Distributing of Erasmus his Ecclesiastes to all the Universities of Great Britain and Ireland, it passed in the Affirmative.

The Report of Mr Anderson concerning Mr James Martin being taken into Consideration, and it being farther reported, that he was willing to afford the whole Number of Erasmus his Ecclesiastes to the Associates at two Shillings and three Pence each, and that he would be concerned no longer in Proposing the Sale of them to the Booksellers; but that he would not part with his Right to the second Impression of the said Book; and a Motion being made, that the Associates do take of him the Number due to the Trustees at two Shillings and three Pence each, it passed in the Affirmative.

A Motion being made, that the Associates do buy the Rest of him at the same Price, to be paid upon Delivery, and that the Delivery be, when the Associates have ready Mony to pay for the same, and in Consideration, that it is uncertain, when that may be, the said Mr James Martin shall have the Liberty of Selling such as are in his own Hands to any Person for his own Advantage, it passed in the Affirmative.

Mr James Martin also mentioned, that the Boxes, in which the Books were, which Dr Bray had given by Will to be sold for fifty Pounds do belong to him as Executor of Dr Bray, being 18 in all, and that they cost the Dr 8s each, but that he would dispose of them for four Shillings each, agreed, that when the Books are sold, Notice be given to the said Mr Martin to fetch the Boxes from the Store Room, because the Associates have no Occasion for them.

Agreed, that Arthur Bedford do write to Mr Bundy, to put him in Mind of waiting on the Bishop of London for a particular Account of the Clergy and Negroes in the several Islands and Plantations in America, and that if Mr Bundy is not at Leasure to do it, that the said Arthur Bedford do wait on the Bishop of London for that Purpose, as soon as he receives an Answer from Mr Bundy.

A Motion being made, that any Associate, who will pay the Summe of four Guineas, instead of a Benefaction or Subscription for the Year last past, to clear the Debts of these Associates upon their Designs in General, and the Overplus to be applied for those things which are wanting to carry on the good Designs of these Associates, and for Binding up of Erasmus his Ecclesiastes, and the Books in the Store Room for Parochial Libraries, or the Plantations, and the Remainder to be also applied for Parochial Libraries, and the Conversion of the Negroes, as there shall be most Occasion, shall have a Library of the Books which are in the Store Room bound, and sent with a Box to any Parish, which he shall nominate, it passed in the affirmative.

A Person having offered to lend these Associates the Summe of an hundred Pounds for the Space of a Year without any Interest, and the Question being put, that his Offer be agreed to, it is ordered to be reconsidered.

John Adderly of the Parish of St Leonard's Shoreditch Weaver, offered himself with his Wife, two Sons and a Daughter to go to the charitable Colony.

Mr James Martin having approved of the Design of these Associates to sell the Books bequeathed by Dr Bray for fifty Pounds to ⟨begin⟩ found a Library in a Market Town to Mr Daniel Somerschald for the Town of Maidstone in the County in Kent, it is agreed that the same be sold to the said Mr Somerschald, provided that the said Library is subjected to the Rules for Preserving Parochial Libraries, according to the Statute of the seventh Year of Queen Anne, and to the Visitation and Direction of these Associates for that Purpose.

The Reverend Mr Fox of Reading having proposed to exchange several of Dr Moore's Theological Works for Allen on the Covenant, Dr Bray's Lectures, and Kettlewell's Practical Believer,[83] which he should distribute for Parochial Libraries and such like pious and charitable Uses, and that he did not insist upon Value for Value, it is agreed, that it be accepted.

A Motion being made, that the Mony in hand toward the Parochial Libraries be laid out in Binding such Books as are in the Store Room, and proper for such a purpose, and that they are sorted into Libraries to be ready to be sent away at the first Order, it passed in the Affirmative, reserving twenty Shillings in Hand to defray the necessary Charges for sending away such Library.

Agreed, that a Paper be printed to be pasted on the Inside of the Title Page of Erasmus his Ecclesiastes in these Words.

Hic liber dicatus est in eorum usum, qui sacros ordines ambiuent, & in Academiâ[84]

Agreed, that Inquiry be made upon what Terms Edwards his Body of Divinity in three Volumes in Folio may be purchased either singly or together, & also the Right of Copy, from the Widow Edwards his Executrix.

A Letter from Mr Hales, and another from Captain Coram to be sent to Weymouth relating to a Parochial Library to be settled there, were read and ordered to be sent forward.

Adjourned to Thursday the ⟨fifteenth⟩ 22d Day of April next.

🙾 At a Meeting of the Associates for Mr D'allone's Charity at Manwarings Coffee House on Thursday the ⟨fifteenth⟩ twenty second Day of April in the Year of our Lord 1731, Mr Oglethorpe in the Chair, there being present Mr Smith and Arthur Bedford.

Adjourned til Thursday the thirteenth Day of May next.[85]

[*Percival, May 4, 1731*]

He [Sir Robert Walpole] then desired the Carolina Company, in which I am concerned, would abate him five hundred tickets of the two thousand lottery tickets he promised us, for the lottery is over full by above thirty thousand tickets, and he was obliged to cut off from the whole in order to please all. I said I would enquire how many we had sold and let him know.[86]

🙾 At a Meeting of the Associates for Mr D'allone's Charity at Manwarings Coffee House on Thursday the thirteenth Day of May in the Year of our Lord 1731. There being present Captain Coram, Mr Smith, and Arthur Bedford.

Adjourned 'til Thursday the twenty seventh Day of May next.

☙ At a Meeting of the Associates at Manwarings Coffee House on Thursday the 27th day of May, Mr Oglethorpe in the Chair, there being present Mr Vernon, Mr Holland, Mr Coram & Samuel Smith.[87]

Mr Oglethorpe pay'd Mr Cholmondley out of the stock of the Associates eleven Pounds eleven Shillings & six Pence for binding three hundred of Erasmus his Ecclesiastes

Agreed, that Samuel Smith do prepare against the next Meeting the Form of a Letter to be sent to the Vice Chancellors of Oxford & Cambridge to acquaint them with the Design of the Associates in Relation to Erasmus his Ecclesiastes

Agreed, that he lays before these Associates at their next Meeting his Account of Dr Bray's Life & Designs

Agreed, that Mr Coram do wait on Mr Page & report his Answer to their Proposal for his binding a Number of Erasmus his Ecclesiastes

Adjourn'd to Thursday the 17th Day of June next

☙ At a Meeting of the Associates at Manwarings Coffee House on Thursday the 17th day of June, Mr Vernon in the Chair, there being present Mr Holland, Mr Hales, Mr Coram & Samuel Smith.

Mr Coram reported that he had seen Mr Page & that Mr Page declines the binding of Erasmus his Ecclesiastes, Binding being no Branch of his Trade

The Form of a Letter prepar'd by Saml. Smith for the Vice Chancellors of Oxford & Cambridge was read & approved Agreed that he do ⟨write &.⟩ send the same

An historical Account was lay'd by him before the Associates of Dr Bray's Life & Designs & with some alterations the whole was approvd.[88]

[*Percival, June 17, 1731*]

I found also that Mr. Oglethorp and the other gentlemen concerned in the Carolina settlement are displeased with the charter as drawn up by the Attorney General, who has constituted a new election of Councillors every three years, which we apprehend is to take the power out of our hands, and put it into new ones, who may convert the scheme into a job. He has also put the Militia of the intended colony into the single hand of the Governor of Carolina, whereby he at his pleasure may distress our people. He has also inserted some words that seem to give the King a duty on the imports and exports of the small traffic they may carry on, which is thought a great discouragement.[89]

꼐§ At a Meeting of the Associates at Manwarings Coffee House on Thursday the 8th Day of July, Mr Oglethorpe in the Chair, there being present Mr Bedford & Samuel Smith.

Agreed that the Associates do meet during the Summer Season at five of the Clock in the Afternoon

Mr Bedford & Saml Smith reported that they had sent two Libraries of fifteen Pounds Value each pursuant to the Directions of the Associates, one to How in the County of Norfolk and the other to Collerne in the County of Wilts

Mr Bedford resign'd his Office as joynt Secretary with Samuel Smith to the Associates

꼐§ At a Meeting of the Associates at Manwarings Coffee House on Thursday the 22 Day of July Mr Vernon in the Chair, there being present Mr Oglethorpe, Mr Hucks Mr Coram & Samuel Smith.

Agreed that a certain Clause in Dr Bray his Will relating to the Sale or Distribution of his Books be lay'd before the Associates at their next Meeting

Agreed that Samuel Smith do attend the Associates at their several Meetings & be desir'd to continue acting as their Secretary

Agreed that Samuel Smith be desir'd to receive the forty Pounds returnd in Part of fifty Pounds for the Library ⟨designed for⟩ to be sent to Maidstone pursuant to an Agreement made by Virtue of Dr. Bray his Will

Agreed that a Clause in Dr Bray his Will vesting four Shares & a Quarter of Share in The Mine Adventure in the Associates be lay'd before the Associates at their next Meeting[90]

Agreed that ⟨Mr⟩ Samuel Smith be desir'd to lay before the Associates at their next Meeting the Draught of a Letter to be sent to the Commissarys & Clergy in America, acquainting them with the Trust created by Dr Bray for the Instruction of the Negroes & desiring their ⟨Concurrence &⟩ Advice in promoting these good Designs

Adjournd til Thursday the 12 of August next

[*Privy Council, August 12, 1731*]

Report of Attorney and Solicitor General with draft charter referred to a Committee.[91]

🕭 At a Meeting of the Associates at Manwarings Coffee House on Thursday the 12 Day of August Mr Oglethorpe in the Chair there being present Mr Anderson & Samuel Smith.

Agreed that Mr Oglethorpe do desire Mrs Godithla Martin, Executrix to the late Dr Bray, to transfer two Shares in the Mine Adventure bequeath'd to the Trustees of Mr D'Allones Bequest, to Mr Adam Anderson.

A Letter from the Revd. Mr Hales signifying Sr William Perkins Desire of a Parochial Library for Chertsey was read [92]
Agreed that Samuel Smith do desire Mr Hales to acquaint Sr Wm with the Rules relating to Parochial Libraries And that his Request will be laid before the Associates at their next Meeting in order to the ratifying their Compliance therewith.

Agreed that Mr Oglethorpe do desire Mr Roger Aldey & his Wife to transfer one Share in the Mine Adventure Company, standing in the Books of the said Company in her Maiden Name, to Mr. Adam Anderson.[93]

Agreed that Mr Anderson be desird to acquaint Sr Hans Sloane that the Trustees desire to present to Him a manuscript Copy of the Life ⟨& Designs⟩ of the late Dr Bray [94]

Paid by Mr. Oglethorp pursuant to a former
Order to Mr. Smith for Disbursements   £. 3: 13: 9
And to Mr. Anderson for Mr. Wainwright   2: 2: -
                                              _____
                                       In all 5: 15: 9

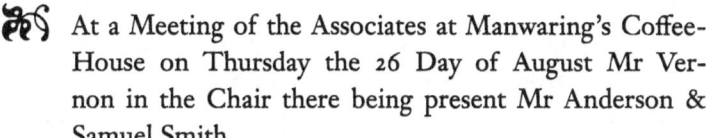 At a Meeting of the Associates at Manwaring's Coffee-House on Thursday the 26 Day of August Mr Vernon in the Chair there being present Mr Anderson & Samuel Smith.

Mr Anderson having reported that the three Shares in the Mine Adventure are transferr'd into his Name was desir'd by the Associates to dispose of them to the best Advantage Sir Wm. Perkins his Request was propos'd a second Time & agreed to & Samuel Smith was order'd to send the Books desir'd.

Jas Vernon

[*Percival, September 7, 1731*]

After this I went to the Bedford Arms Tavern in Covent Garden, to meet the gentlemen concerned in the Carolina Plantation, and

I found there Mr. Oglethorp, Mr. Digby, Mr. Heathcote, Mr. Vernon, Mr. Hucks, and Mr. ———.

We read over the draft of the King's patent constituting our Corporation, and took notes of several objections thereto with the reasons for supporting our objections, which are to be reduced into writing and given to the Attorney General. They filled up some blanks, particularly that I am to be president for the first year, and Mr. Digby chairman.[95]

At a Meeting of the Associates at Manwarings Coffee House on Thursday the 9 Day of September Mr Vernon in the Chair, there being present Mr Anderson & Samuel Smith.

Mr Anderson reported that he had pursuant to a Minute of the 26 Day of August last disposd of the three Shares & 5/116 Parts of a Share in the Mine Adventure Company at the Rate of £.4:10:0. per Share & had expended on that Accot. in all £.2:0:0. So that the Net Proceed of the said Shares amounted to £.11:15:0 which he is desir'd to pay into the Hands of Mr Oglethorpe at the next Meeting

A Letter from the Revd. Mr Samuel Netham of Streatley was read concerning the Security to be given for the Preservation of the Parochial Library.[96]

Agreed, that Mr Samuel Smith do acquaint him that the Associates will readily acquiesce in such Security as the Ordinary approves of.

Adjourn'd to Thursday the 14 Day of October next.

Jas Vernon

At a Meeting of the Associates at Manwarings Coffee House on Thursday the 14th Day of October Mr Oglethorpe in the Chair there being present Mr Vernon Mr Heathcote Captain Coram Mr Anderson. & Samuel Smith.

Read a Letter from the Right Hon. the Lady Elizabeth Hastings dated September 10 & another from Mr Wadsworth of How with an Account of his having receivd a Parochial Library dated August 23

Agreed that Samuel Smith do prepare Answers to them to be layd before the Associates at their next Meeting

Sam Smith acquainted the Associates that he had receivd five Pounds f[ro]m my Lady Hastings & Deliverd the same into the Hands of James Oglethorpe Esq;

Payd by Mr Anderson to James Oglethorpe Esq; eleven Pounds fifteen Shillings mention'd in a former Minute

Agreed that Samuel Smith do wait on Thomas Towers Esq; with the Will of the late Dr Bray to have his Opinion concerning certain Clauses therein.

🕮 At a Meeting of the Associates at Manwarings Coffee house on Thursday the 28 Day of October Mr Vernon in the Chair there being present Lord Percival Captain Coram Mr Heathcote Mr Oglethorpe Mr Hucks & Saml. Smith

Saml Smith reported that a Parochial Library for Buckland in Berkshire of about ten Pounds ten Shillings Value was sent to Mr Burton October 6 & that He acknowledgd his receiving of it in a Letter to the Revd Mr Bedford dated October 14. And also that, pursuant to a former Minute, some Books had been sent to Sr Wm Perkins towards founding a Parochial Library at Chertsey

The Answers prepar'd to the two Letters receiv'd viz one from the Lady Elizabeth Hastings, & the other from the Revd Mr Wadsworth,[97] were approv'd & order'd to be sent

A Letter from the Revd. Mr Holt of Barbadoes dated July 30

was read, but the Consideration of it was referr'd to another Meeting, the Associates esteeming it proper that before they came to any Resolution the Gentleman who brought it shou'd be desir'd to attend

Saml Smith reported that he had waited on Thomas Towers Esq; with the Will of the late Dr Bray & left it with him for his Perusal & Examination

※ At a Meeting of the Associates at Manwarings Coffee House on Thursday the 11 Day of November Mr Hales in the Chair there being present Mr Vernon Mr Anderson Captain Coram Mr. Oglethorpe & Mr. Smith.

The Revd Mr Hales payd into the Hands of Saml Smith fifty Guineas fm a Gentleman & Lady who desire to be unknown for the Use of the Designs of the Associates in general twenty Guineas being given by the Gentleman & thirty by his Lady

Agreed that Mr Hales be desird to return the Thanks of the Associates to both & acquaint them that their Benefactions shall be enterd & applyd as they desire

Agreed that Mr. Oglethorpe be desired to pay into the Hands of Adam Anderson or any other whom he shall think fit As much Money as with the 54 £. to be paid for the 6. pr Cent Annihilation on the 900 £. S. Sea Annties. will make up or replace the said 54.£. South Sea Annuity

Mr Bolton was pleas'd to attend according to the Desire of the Associates & promis'd to give them his Thoughts in Writing at another Meeting [98]

The Revd Mr Hales reported that Sr Wm Perkins had receiv'd the Books wch were sent from the Associates towards founding a Library at Chertsey, that He will have proper Presses made to preserve them in, & that near 100 more Books were already added to them.

Saml. Smith pay'd in the fifty Guineas aforemention'd at Mr Alderman Childs,[99] & placing it as he was directed, to the Account of James Oglethorpe Esq, he deliver'd to Mr Oglethorpe the Note thereof

       Stephen Hales

[*Percival, November 26, 1731*]

Mr. Oglethorpe dined with me. He came to acquaint me that he had hopes the Committee of Council would consent to the alterations we desire may be made in our Carolina Charter to be granted. One is that we desire to be independent of the Governor of Carolina, because it may else be in the power of the Governor to discourage the settlement as it thrives, and may give jealousy to the natives there. Another is, that there be not a rotation of Common Council men, which may throw the management into the hands of corrupt men, who will make an exchange {gradu}ally of the design.[100]

At a Meeting of the Associates at Manwarings Coffee House on Thursday the 9th Day of December, Mr Oglethorpe in the Chair there being present Mr Smith Capt. Coram Mr. Anderson Mr Vernon Mr Hucks & Mr Eyles & Mr Heathcote

Agreed That Mr Smith do desire Mr Hales to preach the Anniversary Sermon on Thursday the 24th Day of February next And that if Mr Hales excuses himself Mr Burton be desir'd to preach the same

⟨Mr Bolton⟩ Sam Smith deliver'd in Mr Bolton his Opinion concerning the most effectual Method of promoting the Conversion of the Negroes in Barbadoes wch was read

Agreed that Saml Smith do prepare an Answer to Mr Holts Letter to be layd before the Associates at their next Meeting Adjourned to Thursday the 13th Day of January next
J Oglethorpe

[*Privy Council, December 14, 1731*]

By a Committee of the Lords of His Majestys most Honoble Privy Council.

His Majesty having been pleased to referr unto this Committee a Draught of a Charter prepared by His Majestys Attorney and Sollicitor Generall for Establishing Colonys in America—and likewise to referr a Petition of the Lord Viscount Percival and others Petitioners for the said Charter praying to be heard upon the said Draught—The Lords of the Committee this day took the said Draught of a Charter into their Consideration and heard the said Petitioners thereupon—and think it proper hereby to referr the following Points to the Lords Commissioners for Trade and Plantations—Vizt

> For Settling a Western Boundary to the Colony to be Establisht by this Charter And for ascertaining the Distance of the Islands upon the Eastern Shore from the Continent.
> As likewise for fixing the Number of Acres proper to be granted to each Person who shall settle there—

Upon which Points the said Lords Commissioners are to hear the Petitioners for the same Charter, and Report to this Committee their Opinion thereupon.
Temple Stanyan [101]

[The Committee] are humbly pleased to refer back the said Draught to Mr. Attorney and Sollicitor General to reconsider the following Points and to make proper alterations and to insert proper Clauses therein and lay the same before this Committee as soon as conveniently they can Vizt.

That at the end of the Blank left for the Names of the present Corporation words be inserted to include the Members hereafter to be Elected—

That as it is intended this Corporation should not extend to the settling any other Colony than that of Georgia in South Carolina, so the Title and other parts of this Draught are to be made correspondent thereto.—

It being the opinion of the Committee that the Common Council men to be appointed should be continued during their good behaviour—That therefore all Clauses relating to a New Choice by way of Rotation be left out or made conformable to this opinion.

That as the Members of the Corporation are no more at present than twenty one It is proposed that the Number of Common Council men should be no more than fifteen. But in regard it is expected the numbers of the Corporation will be encreased to a greater Number. A Clause is therefore to be inserted Directing that as soon as the said Members shall be encreased, That the Number of Common Council men should by Election be augmented to twenty one.

That a Clause be added to restrain the Members of the Corporation from having any Grants of Land made to themselves or to any others in trust for them—

And that another Clause be added to declare all Grants of Land to be made by the Corporation in this Colony Void unless such Grants shall be registered within a limited time, with the Auditor of the Plantations.[102]

[*Board of Trade and Plantations, December 17, 1731*]

Mr. Oglethorpe and Mr. Towers two of the Gentlemen concerned in the Petition considered at this Board the 3rd of December 1730 desiring a Charter of Incorporation for settling poor people in South Carolina attending, an order of the Committee of Council dated the 14th Inst referring to the Board of Trade some points relating to a Charter for Establishing Colonies in South Carolina was read. And their Lordships after some discourse with Mr. Oglethorpe upon this Subject agreed to propose to the Lords of the Committee as follows Vizt. That the Western bounds of the said Grant should extend as far as the Western Bounds of Carolina. That all the Islands to the Eastward of this Grant between the Rivers Savannah and Alatamaha and within the distance of Twenty Leagues from the Shore should be included in the Grant and That the said Corporation should not be Impowered to grant above 500 Acres to any one person. The Board then gave directions for preparing the Draft of a Report accordingly [103]

[*Board of Trade and Plantations, December 22, 1731*]

To the Rt Honble. the Lords of the Committee of His Majestys most Honble. Privy Council
My Lords
  In Pursuance of your Lordships Order of the 14th of this Month, referring to us the following Points *vizt* The settling a western Boundary to the Colony to be established in So. Carolina, by Virtue of a Charter petitioned for by the Lord Percival & others; and for ascertaining the Distance of the Islands upon the Eastern Shore from the Continent; as likewise for fixing the Number of Acres proper to be granted to each Person who shall settle there
  We have been attended by ⟨Mr. Oglethorpe & Mr. Towers, Two⟩ some of the Petitioners, and take Leave to represent to your Lordships, that We think the western Boundary of this new Charter may extend as far as that described in the ancient Patents granted by King Charles 2d. to the late Lords Proprietors of Carolina,

whereby that Province was allowed to extend *Westward in a direct Line as far as the So. Seas.*

With Respect to the Islands upon the Eastern Shore from the Continent, We think this new Charter may include all such as lie opposite to & *within Twenty Leagues of the Coast* between the Rivers Savanah & Alatamaha, which are not already inhabited or settled by any Authority deriv'd from the Crown; and as to the Quantity of Land to be granted to each Person who shall settle within the Limits of the Charter, We are humbly of Opinion that the Proprietors should be restrained from granting above five hundred Acres to any one Person.

         We are, My Lords, &c.
Whitehall   P Docminique
Decr. 22 1731   T Pelham
         O Bridgeman [104]

※ At a Meeting of the Associates at Manwarings Coffee-House on Thursday the 13 Day of January Mr Vernon in the Chair there being present Mr Anderson Mr Coram & Mr Oglethorpe

Agreed That Sam Smith do write to Mr Burton & return him the Thanks of the Associates for his Letter of January 2 And acquaint him that they accept of his kind offer to preach at their ensuing Anniversary

The Answer prepard to Mr Holts Letter being read was approv'd & order'd to be sent

Two Letters from the Commissary of Maryland to Sam Smith were read wherein were inclos'd his Address to the Clergy of that Province at his late Visitation & his Proceedings in relation to the Conversion of the Negroes [105]

Agreed that a Parcel of the Bp of London his Letters to the Masters & Mistresses of Families & to the Value of five Pounds be sent to the Commissary

Agreed that Sam Smith do prepare an Answer to the Commissary his Letters to be lay'd before the Associates at their next Meeting

[*Privy Council, January 19, 1732*]

{Committee for Plantation Affairs, having considered the draft of a charter} for Establishing a New Colony in the Province of South Carolina by the name of Georgia in America . . . and having filled up the Severall Blanks left therein and made such Alterations as they Judged most proper for answering the ends proposed thereby Do Agree humbly to lay the said Draught before Your Majesty as proper for Your Royal approbation.[106]

[*Percival, January 19, 1732*]

Went . . . after dinner to the Committee of Council, which sat upon our charter for settling colonies in America. The Lords of the Council there present were the Lord President, Earl of Marchmont, Lord Torrington, Sir William Strickland, Horace Walpole and Earl of Islay. They approved the charter as altered, and we concerned therein acquiesced in their pleasure, though against the grain.[107]

[*Percival, January 21, 1732*]

. . . I went with the other trustees for the Carolina Colony to see a house proper for keeping our office in.[108]

[*Privy Council, January 27, 1732*]

Upon reading at the Board a Report from the Lords of the Committee of His Majestys most Honoble Privy Council for Plantations Affairs dated the 19th of this Instant upon the Draught of

a Charter for Establishing a New Colony in His Majestys Province of South Carolina by the name of the Colony of Georgia in America which Draught the said Lords of the Committee humbly Offered to His Majty. as proper for his Royal Approbation, —His Majesty this day took the said Report and Draught of a Charter into his Consideration and is thereupon pleased with the Advice of His privy Council to approve of the said Draught (which is hereunto annexed) and to Order as it is hereby Ordered that His Grace the Duke of Newcastle His Majestys Principal Secretary of State do Cause a Warrant to be prepared for His Majestys Royal Signature for passing the Same under the Great Seal of Great Britain.
A true Copy
W: Sharpe [109]

⁂ At a Meeting of the Associates at Manwarings Coffee-House on Thursday January 27 Mr Oglethorpe in the Chair there being present Mr Vernon Mr Hales Mr Anderson Mr Coram

The Revd. Mr Hales having Some Time Since paid into Mr. Anderson's hands Six pounds, being the Surplus Money of the Interest of the 900 £. South Sea Annuities of Mr. Dallones Trust, after paying Mr. Martin's £.30. for one Year at Micha[elma]s. Last, & Mr. Anderson having been impowered to receive the 6. pr. Cent Annihilation on the said £.900. Annuities being £.54. has Since by order of this Meeting replaced the Said £.54. Annuity Stock, at the Price of £.59: 2: 4d. & did now deliver up the Remaining Money into Mr. Oglethorp's. Hands being Seventeen Shillings & Six pence.

The Revd. Mr. Hales did now pay into Mr. Oglethorp's hands £50, formerly put into his Hands by an unknown Benefactress as mentiond in a former Minute of - - - For Purchasing proper Books for the Conversion of the Negroe Slaves.

Sam Smith receiv'd of James Oglethorpe Esq; the Sum of five

Pounds wch was directed to be lay'd out in purchasing a Number of the Bp of London his Letters to Masters & Mistresses to be sent to the Commissary of Maryland pursuant to a Minute of the last Meeting.

The Answer prepard by Sam Smith to the Letters of the Commissary of Maryland was approv'd & order'd to be sent

[*Percival, February 4, 1732*]

Met our Carolina gentlemen, and prepared a draft of an account of our design in order to be printed.[110]

[*Percival, February 9, 1732*]

This morning, at nine a clock, I went to Mr. Hucks, in Great Russell Street, where by appointment came Mr. Oglethorp, Mr. Digby, Mr. Heathcot, Mr. More, and Mr. Eyles. From thence we went to wait on the Duke of Newcastle in Lincoln's Inn Fields, to desire him to move the King to sign the warrant for our Carolina Charter, which he promised.[111]

At a Meeting of the Associates at Manwaring's Coffee-House on Thursday February 10 Mr Oglethorpe in the Chair there being present Mr Vernon Mr Hales Mr Anderson Captain Coram Mr Belitha[112]

Samuel Smith pay'd into the Hands of Mr Anderson the Sum of fifty Pounds remitted fm the Rev Mr Netter[?] of Maidstone for the Books of the late Dr Bray by the Order of the Associates

Agreed That Mr Oglethorpe be desir'd to advance & He did advance accordingly five Pounds seven Shillings & six Pence out of the Stock of the Associates to purchase with the said Sum fifty Pounds South Sea Annuities

Agreed That Mr Anderson be desir'd to purchase for the Associates fifty Pounds South Sea Annuities with the said Sum of fifty five Pounds seven Shillings and six Pence

Sam Smith reported that he had bought two hundred & fifty of the Bp of London's Letters to Masters & Mistresses & with the five Pounds given him by Mr Oglethorpe for that Purpose & had sent them by Captain Anderson to the Commissary of Maryland

Agreed That a thousand Summonses be printed against the Anniversary Sermon & Sent to the several Associates

Agreed That two Guineas be payd to Sam Smith for defraying the Charges on Account of the Associates & they were payd by Mr Oglethorpe accordingly

James Oglethorpe

[*Percival, February 17, 1732*]

I promised to go this day sennit to Bow Church in Cheapside to the annivarsary sermon left by Dr. Bray for recommending the charity left by Mr. Dalone for converting negroes, after which we are to dine at Brawn's eating house.[113]

[*Percival, February 18, 1732*]

Perceiving an unaccountable delay in the putting his Majesty's seal to the Georgia Charter, and that it sticks with the Duke of Newcastle, all our gentlemen concerned as trustees are much out of humour and some are for flinging it up, and restoring the money arising from the lottery tickets which were given up to tell for the advantage of the colony. I told my mind freely to Horace Walpole, sitting by him this morning, that we thought ourselves ill used, and that if it was expected by the Government that we should entreat any more the passing this charter, he was mistaken, for it is a matter we think they ought to entreat us to undertake; that being restrained at our own desire by oath from making any advantage directly or indirectly of the charter, this delay must be the highest reflection on us as if we did not intend to regard our oaths, for this delay cannot possibly be given but from a suspicion we should abuse our trust. If, therefore, he did not think it a good thing, I desired he would tell us, and we would quit it. He replied, he thought it a good thing, but—as he was going on, a gentleman took him behind the chair to discourse him, and I lost the satisfaction of knowing whence the delay arose.

Soon after, Mr. Oglethorp came to me, and said that upon his complaining to Drummond of the usage,[114] Drummond replied, Sir Robert was very hearty for the charter, but that it happened the day before we waited on the Duke of Newcastle to desire he would forward the King's signing the charter, his Grace had carried the charter in a bag with five other things for his Majesty to sign, but that the King not being in right humour, refused to sign any one of them, and that the Duke is a person of that timorous nature, as to be a great while resolving to take fresh opportunities of furthering things he has met with a rebuff in. John Drummond is a director of the bank, and member of our House.

Next Thursday, Dr. Bray's anniversary sermon is to be preached by Mr. Burton, of Oxford, a very ingenious acquaintance of Mr. Oglethorp's, at Bow Church in Cheapside. I earnestly pressed that he should be instructed to say nothing reproachful to the Government for retarding the charter so long as eighteen months, but to speak of it as a thing that will succeed, and show the benefit of it.[115]

[*Percival, February 24, 1732*]

This morning I went to St. Bride's Church to hear Mr. Burton, of Oxford, preach an excellent sermon in favour of Christian education of youth, of the conversion of negroes, and of the savage Indians. He showed the indispensable duty of kings and magistrates from Scripture, reason and human policy to take care of religion and further it in proper methods of educating youth, and towards the close spoke of our design to settle colonies in South Carolina, handsomely commending the King for approving it. We were about twenty-five persons favourers of this design, who after sermon dined at Brawn's in the City, the chief of whom were Sir William Chaplin, Sir Gilbert Heathcote, Sir Philip Parker, etc., and about a dozen other Parliament men.[116]

But I was sorry to learn from Mr. Drummond that the charter still sticks, though the Duke of Newcastle has promised to carry it on the first occasion to his Majesty for to put the seal to it. He told me he was with Sir Robert Walpole this morning, and told him how uneasy we all were that such delays are used in putting the seal, and that we thought the Ministry used us very ill to imagine we would still entreat for a charter as if we had some advantage to gain by it, whereas it ought rather to be expected by us that the Government should entreat us to accept it. Sir Robert replied, "Mr. Drummond, the gentlemen wrong me to believe the charter sticks with me, and they wrong the Duke in thinking it sticks with him. It is not proper for me to tell you where it sticks."

Hereupon I asked if his Majesty did not like the terms of the charter. Mr. Drummond replied he believed some things must be altered in it. Then, said I, I am resolved to have no more to do with it, nor will the other gentlemen; but I beg you not to tell them what Sir Robert said to you, for I would not have them know this of the King. He said he did not intend to tell them, because they were warm men, but to me he thought it proper, because I took things coolly.

Certainly the King should have taken his resolution before he had suffered the thing to go so far. The gentlemen lay all the fault on the Ministry, as a pitiful revenge on them for voting against the salt duty, as I think all the trustees designed by the charter have done except myself.[117]

[*Percival, February 25, 1732*]

When at the House, Mr. Spence, the Serjeant-at-Arms, came to me, and taking me aside told me the Duke of Newcastle had sent him to me to assure me that he was desirous the Carolina Charter might pass in the manner we desired, but that the King had made an objection to the signing it, namely, that by the charter as drawn, we the trustees, had reserved to them the nomination of the officers of the Militia. That since by the charter the approbation of the Governor, nominated by us, is in the King, his Majesty thought it reasonable the Governor should nominate the inferior officers. His Grace therefore desired to know of me what objections I had to it that he might fairly lay them before the King. I answered Mr. Spence in the manner following: That I desired my thanks might be returned to his Grace for his good disposition to forward the charter, that I had for some time perceived a delay put to the signing our charter, and should be very glad to know if there was really a design to grant it, for if his Majesty in his great wisdom and reflection had found difficulties he did not think of till now, I should for my own part acquiesce in his Majesty's judgment and resign my part in it, as I believed many other gentlemen concerned in it would do. That I was but one man, and could not take upon me to give reasons for insisting on what now appeared a difficulty, for the other gentlemen might support the charter in the form now drawn with better arguments than I on the sudden could offer, but I wished Mr. Spence would speak to Mr. Oglethorp, Mr. Hucks, Mr. Heathcot, or other gentlemen, and hear what they have to say.

When we parted, I called the members who I could find in the House together, namely, Mr. Towers, Mr. Digby, Mr. Holland, Mr. Oglethorp, Mr. La Roche, and Mr. Hucks, and after telling them what had passed between Mr. Spence and me, with my answer, which they much approved, we agreed to desire Mr. Spence to walk up to us in the Speaker's chamber,[118] which he did; and we gave him the reasons why we could not accept the charter on his Majesty's conditions; our reasons were, that our colony will be for many years in an infant state, and not able to support the different characters of civil and military offices, so that the civil officer must be the same with the military, but if one person must have two masters, namely, the trustees in the civil and the Governor of Carolina in the military, we conceived the affair of settling a colony could not proceed on our scheme. That so much expense attended his Majesty's granting employments, we should not be able to defray it, not to mention the time lost in attending the Government to get commissions out, which we, the trustees, should do without loss of time or expense. That the charter had twice received his Majesty's approbation, and all difficulties started either removed or yielded to; finally, that we were from the beginning of opinion that the less our colony were dependent on the Governor of Carolina there, better success there was to expect. Mr. Spence said he would tell the Duke what we said.

After this Mr. Oglethorp came to me and said the gentlemen were desirous I should speak to Sir Robert Walpole about it, by which we should know whether the King or the Ministry were the obstructors of our charter. I said I would, but afterwards meeting Mr. Drummond, I told him I thought it proper to acquaint the gentlemen that the charter stops with the King, seeing the Duke of Newcastle had declared so, by which means Sir Robert Walpole, who is not in fault (but yet thought so) would be exculpt, and therefore if he pleased I would let them know what had passed between him and Sir Robert yesterday. He agreed to it, and accordingly I told Mr. Oglethorp and Mr. Holland of it. Then said they, there's an end of the charter, and Sir Robert is the faulty person. I could only say he affirmed not, but they would not believe the King would invent new scruples, after having advanced so far.[119]

[*Percival, February 27, 1732*]

This day I drew up reasons why the trustees of the Georgia Settlement cannot agree to the Governor of Carolina's naming the officers of the Militia, which paper, if the trustees approve, shall be conveyed to the King.[120]

[*Percival, February 28, 1732*]

... repaired to the House, where I showed to several gentlemen of our Carolina Colony the paper of reasons I drew up why we could not consent to the Governor of Carolina's naming our Militia officers. They much approved it, but last of all meeting Mr. Oglethorp, he told me that he was yesterday to wait on the Lord President to acquaint him with what had passed between the Duke of Newcastle and us, and that the Lord President told him the matter was too far gone, so that the King could not make any more objections to the powers given us by the charter without acting against law. So I believe we shall not give any paper of reasons, it being unnecessary.[121]

[*Percival, March 2, 1732*]

Mr. Spence acquainted me this day that the Duke of Newcastle had desired him to assure me that he had used all the arguments with the King he could think of to sign the charter in the manner we desired it, but that the King took him up very short and angrily, but he would urge it to his Majesty once more. I desired Mr. Spence to thank his Grace for the assurance he gave us of his desire to make the charter succeed, and that he would speak again to his Majesty, and to tell his Grace that we were very desirous to see an end to it one way or other.

. . . .

Mr. Oglethorp told me he had seen my paper of reasons for insisting on our charter as at present drawn, which he much approved, but he thought the fourth reason, though absolutely true, would not be fit to offer, since the very reason why the charter stops is the thing we insist upon in that article.[122]

[*Percival, March 3, 1732*]

This morning I visited Mr. Horace Walpole. I told him of the stop that is made of the Carolina grant; that we apprehended there was still a distrust that we sought our private advantage in it, whereas we had no view but serving the public, and I did not know how we came to be such knight-errants. I gave him substantial reasons why we could not depart from the purport of the charter as it now stands, particularly the point the King objects to, namely the Governor of Carolina's naming the inferior officers of the Militia, and that it would be good to tell us soon whether the King is resolved not to pass it without that alteration, that we might return the money we made of the Government Lottery tickets, being resolved not to accept the charter with that alteration. He replied that he knew not one of the Ministry who were against the charter, but this was the King's own objection, he being jealous of his prerogative, but he hoped it would be got over and believed it, that he thought we could make no private advantage of the design, the guards are so strong against it by the charter, though indeed they did think so at first. I said I understood the King could not alter the charter, it having passed the Council, where he was present; he replied, "Yes, the King might by referring it back to be considered in Council." He desired I would not say all this to Oglethorp or the other gentlemen concerned with me, because they were warm men.[123]

[*Percival, March 10, 1732*]

... being three a clock, I and several gentlemen concerned in the intended Carolina Colony, went to the Bedford Arms Tavern in Covent Garden to dine, and take some resolution what to do upon the delay used in granting the charter. The company were Mr. Digby, Mr. Hucks, Mr. Oglethorp, Mr. La Roche, Mr. Heathcot, Captain Gyles [Eyles], Mr. Holland, Mr. Towers, junior, and Mr. Moore. I acquainted them that this morning in the House, Sir Robert Walpole, of his own accord, protested that what we suspected, namely, that the King's objection to signing the charter, was so far from being owing to him, that he was astonished when he heard it; that there were times when things could be done, other times when they could not, but he would take the proper time to get the King to sign. I desired he would allow me to acquaint the gentlemen with what he told me, which he allowed me. After debating the matter, we agreed to wait his Majesty's pleasure, and that any of us, as we had opportunity, should speak to the Ministry for a speedy resolution on that affair, and to give our reasons why we pressed it, without giving reasons why we complied not with his Majesty's present sentiments.[124]

[*Percival, March 14, 1732*]

Dean Berkeley came to see me. . . . I asked him if, having laid aside his Bermuda scheme, he would care to turn over to our Carolina Settlement some part of the subscriptions that were made to his scheme, believing that he might influence many of the subscribers to bestow their intended gifts to what other good projects he would recommend to them.[125]

[*Percival, March 16, 1732*]

From thence I went to Sir Robert Walpole's, where I asked him if his Majesty had taken any resolution for signing our charter. Sir Robert replied he had been so taken up he had no time yet to speak to the King, but he would as soon as possible. I told him he should not be surprised we were so pressing, and gave him sundry reasons for it.¹²⁶

※ At a Meeting of the Associates at Manwaring's Coffee House on Thursday March 23 Mr Hales in the Chair there being present Mr Belitha Mr Anderson Mr Coram Mr Bedford Mr Fox Mr Digby & Sam. Smith.¹²⁷

Mr Anderson reported that he had purchasd fifty Pounds South Sea Annuities pursuant to a Minute of the tenth of February last & deliver'd the Receipt for the same to Mr Oglethorpe

A Letter from the Rev. Mr Preston of Weymouth to the Rev Mr Hales was read desiring a Parochial Library

Agreed that a Library be sent to the Rev. Mr Preston at Weymouth & that the Rev. Mr Bedford & Sam. Smith do prepare the same

Stephen Hales.

[*Percival, April 4, 1732*]

I went to Sir Robert Walpole's levée, who assured me he had laboured, was labouring, and would labour to get the King to sign our Carolina Charter.¹²⁸

[*Percival, April 23, 1732*]

Mr. Sharp, Clerk of the Council, told me that our Carolina Charter had been signed by his Majesty Friday last, but that the Duke of Newcastle desired first to know whether we would not have the time appointed for filling up the number of trustees to 24 altered; for in the charter as it now stands, the time required is on Tuesday the second or third week in February, which time being lapsed by the delay of the charter, we cannot do it till February of next year, but if we would have the date altered to some day of this or the next month, his Grace was ready to do it, but then the charter must be new drawn. Mr. Sharp added that Mr. Oglethorp and others of the trustees having been consulted thereon, replied they were willing to let the charter proceed as it stands, though we cannot fill up our number till next year. Their reason was that if the charter be altered it must go again to the Council and occasion a further delay which might endanger the loss of the charter, at least for this year. I told him and Mr. Holland, as also Mr. La Roche, who I saw soon after, that it put a great hardship on the 15 trustees,[129] to be obliged to act a twelvemonth almost without filling up their number to 24, as required by the charter, because it was on supposition of that complete number that the charter requires a quorum of eight trustees, which being more than half the body, will be hard to find to meet together, because of sickness or necessary avocations. They said it was true, but the chief of our business for a twelvemonth will be only to get in subscriptions and settle schemes for our proceeding, which may be left to committees. I granted it will be a great while before we can proceed to anything of good purpose, because without a necessary fund of money we can do nothing, and I said that under 12,000*l.* we could not undertake to send families over lest we should starve them, for the estimate ought to be made in the highest manner, because of many disappointments we should meet with, and a good stock of money remain for contingencies and unforeseen accidents. I told them Captain Coram, who knew the West Indies well, had declared to me that we could not set out under 12,000*l.* Mr. La Roche agreed we could not under 10,000*l.* I said that was too little, for every family will stand us in 100*l.* at 20*l.* a head the bare fitting out with tools, clothes and transporting, besides which we were to maintain them in provisions a year when arrived, to build houses, etc., and erect a sort of fort, etc.[130]

[*Percival, April 24, 1732*]

This morning Sir Robert Walpole told me the King had signed the charter.[131]

🕮 At a Meeting of the Associates at Manwaring's Coffee-House on Thursday April 27 Mr Vernon in the Chair there being present Mr Hales Mr Bedford Mr Anderson Mr Coram & Sam. Smith

A Letter was read from Mr Fox of Reading desiring of the Associates two Sets of Dr Bray's Lectures for carrying on the Design of erecting Parochial Libraries in these Parts[132]

Agreed That they be sent him accordingly

Agreed That the sending of Erasmus his Ecclesiastes to the Universities of England & Ireland be consider'd the next Meeting of the Associates at which Mr Oglethorpe is present

Agree'd That Sam Smith do buy a Set of Dr More's Works provided he can have them as he apprehends for nine or ten Shillings[133]

Jas Vernon

[*Percival, April 27, 1732*]

I then met the gentlemen concerned in the Carolina Settlement, and we agreed to go in a body to thank Sir Robert Walpole and Lord Wilmington next Thursday for their assistance in forwarding the charter.[134]

[*Percival, May 2, 1732*]

This Morning Mr. Robert Finley, a broken banker many years ago, came to me and expressed his desire of being employed as agent for the Georgia Colony affairs, he designing to go to Carolina and settle there. I replied, that though I am honoured with being named the first in the charter, yet I as yet knew less of the intentions of the gentlemen concerned with me than others, who have pursued the obtaining the charter. That I heard them say, they knew a gentleman of that Colony who was a proper man for to be our agent, and I thought a person settled there of long time was properer than a stranger to that country, such as Mr. Finley is. He replied he was going over to live there, and carry on merchandise before autumn. I answered I could say nothing to it, being but one of many, and that he should speak to others; that I did not see it was worth his while, we hoping to get persons to serve us without profit. He said the reputation of the thing was a great deal to a merchant. I answered I could mention it to the gentlemen, but was resolved to restrain myself as much as possible from influencing them in the measures we shall pursue, other than to see that we carry our affairs with prudence and honesty.

After this, I waited on Mr. La Roche, where, by appointment, I met Mr. Digby, Mr. More, Mr. Holland, Mr. Hucks, and Mr. Oglethorp, and went with them to Sir Robert Walpole's to thank him for the charter granted us. It was agreed I should do it in all their names, and accordingly I said to him as follows: "Sir Robert, the gentlemen concerned in sending colonies to Carolina are come to wait on you, and return you their thanks in behalf of the public for your care and favour in dispatching their charter, and they hope for the continuance of your protection as often as they shall have occasion to apply to you."

Sir Robert answered: He was glad we had obtained the charter, and wished we had it sooner. I answered, we knew it had not stuck with him.

Then we withdrew, and went to wait on my Lord Wilmington, to return him likewise our thanks, but he was abroad.[135]

[*Percival, May 3, 1732*]

I went with the Common Council gentlemen of the Georgia Charter to wait on my Lord Wilmington and the Speaker to thank them for their favour in forwarding the grant. We were eight in number. Mr. Oglethorp, La Roche, Holland, Hucks, Heathcot, Captain Eyles and Mr. Digby. Lord Wilmington said he should always contribute to support the design, and wished it might prove a pattern for all future new settlements in America, if such a number of gentlemen might be found who would give their service for nothing to the public.

The Speaker was gone to the House before we got to his door, but we left our names there.[136]

[*Percival, May 10, 1732*]

Mr. Heathcot told me at the House that he had communicated our scheme (of taking vagrants from the London parishes and binding them apprentices to invalid soldiers to be sent to Carolina, provided the Government gave us the allowance for a certain number of years paid to those invalids, and 10*l*. a head for the vagrants and poor children we transport over) to Mr. Pultney, Mr. Sands, and Sir John Rushout, who were extremely well pleased with it; and Mr. Oglethorp told me he had communicated the same to Sir Robert Walpole and to the Speaker, who were equally pleased with it. They added that they found no disposition in the House to oppose a motion for addressing the King out of the next Acts of Parliament to grant 10,000 for this purpose, grounded on a petition from some parish overseers to be eased of the great number of vagrants and orphan poor in this city.[137]

At a Meeting of the Associates at Manwaring's Coffee House on Thursday May 11 Lord Percival in the Chair there being present Mr Vernon Mr Towers Mr Hucks

Mr Hales Mr Bedford Mr Oglethorpe Mr Heathcote Mr Eyles Captain Coram Mr Holland Mr More Mr Digby & Samuel Smith.

A Benefaction of five Pounds was paid in f[ro]m The Revd Mr Randolf to be apply'd as the Associates shall judge most proper, mentioning that the Charity he had most at heart was the Propagation of the Christian Religion

Agreed That Mr Oglethorpe do return him the Thanks of the Associates for the same

Agree'd, That the Consideration of sending Erasmus his Ecclesiastes be adjourn'd to the next Meeting

Percival

[*Percival, May 11, 1732*]

This morning I went to Sir Robert Walpole to take my leave upon going into the country. He asked me whether Mr. Oglethorp had disposed the angry chiefs of the minority to relish our design of planting colonies in Carolina, and to give the money desired by us for carrying it on. I told him he had. He said the King had given his consent. . . .

Then I went to the House, where some of our gentlemen showed me the motion which was intended to be made to the House tomorrow for addressing his Majesty to give a sum not exceeding 10,000*l.* for binding vagrants and beggars out apprentices at 10*l.* per head, and to allow masters 20*l.* for every four apprentices he should so take, and to settle them in Carolina, the same to be repaid out of the next Acts of Parliament, which motion I approved.

. . . At five o'clock I went to Manwaring Coffee House in Fleet Street, by appointment, to meet my fellow trustees, and deliberate on that motion and other affairs relating to the colony. . . .

. . . But our chief affair was to discuss the motion that is to be made to-morrow, which is to follow several petitions that will be delivered from the inhabitants of Westminster, Southwark, the Tower Hamlets, etc., to be relieved against the great number of vagrants and beggars.

Mr. Oglethorp acquainted us that the motion I saw in the morning had been altered by the Speaker, who said it was contrary to form and order that the House in their address should mention a sum to his Majesty, which ought to be left to him. We considered the motion as thus altered by the Speaker, and finding objections to it, mended it anew: in doing which we spent above three hours. Our great care was that by the wording we might not give encouragement to foreign Protestants to crowd too fast upon us, in expectation of being sent to Carolina, and at the same time not to tie up our hands by resolution of Parliament so strictly as that we might not have the liberty to send some foreigners thither, which will be necessary to carry on the silk growing, the making wine, etc., and we had a debate whether the motion as it stood altered by the Speaker, did allow us to engage with masters to take apprentices; besides, the motion did not express that these apprentices were to be sent to the uncultivated parts of Carolina. These considerations made us alter the motion in such a manner as we judged would answer these ends, and be agreeable to the House.[138]

[*Percival, May 12, 1732*]

This day several petitions were offered to the House, complaining of the great abuses and mischief arising from vagrants and beggars who have no settlement. It was intended by Mr. Oglethorp and the other gentlemen concerned in the new intended settlement of colonies in South Carolina to ground thereupon a motion for addressing the King to grant 10,000*l.* to us for transporting those vagrants and beggars under the age of sixteen to South Carolina, and bind them apprentices to masters we should send over; but an unexpected opposition arose against us, and the House after an hour's debate resolved to go into a Committee of the whole House Wednesday next, to consider the petitions, and how those vagrants may be rendered useful at home.

Captain Vernon and others said we wanted hands in England, and to send vagrants under sixteen years old to America, was a bad scheme for the public. . . .

Sir Gilbert Heathcot, Mr. Heathcot, Mr. Oglethorp spoke on the other side, and showed the advantages of our scheme, and Sir Robert Walpole acquainted the House that the King had been acquainted with it and made no objection; nevertheless the House (though they commended it in general) would not agree to it, so for want of money I find we shall be able to do nothing in pursuance of our charter this year.[139]

[*Percival, May 17, 1732*]

Went to town at the desire of our Associates for sending Colonies to America, to attend the Committee of the whole House, to whom the petitions concerning vagrants were referred; they were in hopes that if a debate arose, the House might be brought to incline to give us 10,000*l*. for carrying on our design, but when the order of the day was called for, the Committee was put off for three weeks in order to lay aside the matter till next year.[140]

At a Meeting of the Associates at Manwaring's Coffee House on Thursday May 25 Mr Vernon in the Chair there being present Mr Hales Mr Coram & Sam Smith Mr Oglethorpe

Three Pounds were paid into the Hands of James Oglethorpe Esq; being the Surplus arising out of the South-Sea Annuity for educating the Negroes, wch was due to the Associates at Lady-Day last

Ja: Vernon

[*Percival, May 29, 1732*]

I received a letter from Mr. Oglethorp that the charter of Georgia settlement had passed all the Offices, and that the Duke of Newcastle has forgiven his fees.[141]

[*Percival, May 30, 1732*]

I went to wait on the trustees of the Georgia Company to return the Duke of Newcastle our thanks for not requiring his fees for passing the charter. He told us it was not his fault it was not dispatched sooner, and promised to assist us in the prosecution of our design. We then waited on my Lord Carteret with a fair copy of the charter, and claimed his promise of concurring with his Majesty, for he is proprietor of one-eighth part of Carolina, and his consent was necessary; he promised his consent again, and gave us good advice how to proceed, particularly he thought we could not set out without at first sending a thousand men which, at 20*l.* a head, comes to 20,000*l.* That we ought to send them by way of regiments subject to martial law. He said he would assist us with his advice, and meet us at any time, for besides the public service, he had a good interest in the success, being possessed of a tract of land 80 miles long on the coast and 300 the other way. His knowledge of that country, and excellent sense on all matters of this nature, gave us great expectations of benefiting by the assistance he was so ready and desirous to give us. He said the Parliament ought to give 30,000*l.* a year out of the Sinking Fund for so great a purpose, on which we might have 300,000*l.* advanced at 3 per cent.[142]

 At a Meeting of the Associates at Manwaring's Coffee House on Thursday June 8th Mr Oglethorpe in the Chair there being present Mr Holland Mr Coram Mr Hales Mr Bedford Mr Vernon Mr Heathcote Mr Hucks Mr Towers & Sam Smith

Mr Coram presented a Paper containing a Draught of the Designs of the Trustees.

Agree'd That it be taken into farther Consideration

Agree'd that Mr Oglethorpe be desir'd to take an House near Old Palace Yard belonging to Mr Blackerby for one Year at a Rent not exceeding thirty Pounds the Landlord to stand to all Taxes Repairs & Charges during the said Term [143]

Agree'd That fourscore of Erasmus his Ecclesiastes be sent the Beginning of next Week directed to Dr Mawson Vice Chancellor of Cambridge at Bennet College And Mr Hales is desir'd to write to give him Notice of their being sent.[144]

A Commission for Collecting Contributions for the Colony of Georgia was read & approv'd & order'd to be engrav'd.

James Oglethorpe

At a Meeting of the Trustees at Waghern's Coffee-House on Thursday June 15 Mr Oglethorpe in the Chair there being present Mr Anderson Mr Coram Mr Bedford Mr Holland Mr Vernon & Samuel Smith

Samuel Smith reported that he had sent fourscore of Erasmus's Ecclesiastes to Dr Mawson Vice-Chancellor of Cambridge pursuant to a Minute of the last Meeting

Mr Oglethorpe was desir'd to pay to Mr Bedford the Sum of four Pounds six Shillings being in full of all Demands to this Day & he pay'd it accordingly

James Oglethorpe

At a Meeting of the Trustees at their Office in Palace Court on Thursday June 22 Mr Oglethorpe in the Chair there being present Mr Hucks Mr Vernon Mr Heathcote Mr Holland Mr Hales Mr Laroche Mr Coram Lord Percival Mr Towers & Sam Smith

A Letter was read from Mr Blackerby No 1 specifying the Agreement for this House

Agreed, that Mr Oglethorpe be desird to take the said House for one Year certain on the Terms proposd clear of parochial & all other Taxes & with a Liberty of renewing for three or seven Years at the Option of the Trustees

Mr Hales pay'd in an hundred Pounds, being a Benefaction from Mrs Elways Wife of Robert Elways Esq;[145] one Moiety to be apply'd to the Uses of the Colony & the other Moiety to the Support of the ⟨Establish'd⟩ Christian Religion there

Agree'd, that Mr Hales be desird to return the Thanks of the Trustees

James Oglethorpe

[*Percival, June 22, 1732*]

We met in our new house, taken for a year certain, with liberty to continue if we like it. We pay only 30*l.* a year, and not manner of taxes. Our landlord is Justice Blackerby. It stands in a lane that goes out of the street that leads from Palace Yard to Milbank ferry. . . .

They were busy setting down the names of the Aldermen of London in order to apply to them for subscriptions to promote the colony.[146]

At a Meeting of the Trustees in Palace Court on Thursday June 29 Mr Oglethorpe in the Chair, there being present the Right Hon. the Lord Percival, Mr Vernon, Mr Holland, Mr Hucks, Mr Laroche, Mr Hales, Mr Anderson, Mr Coram, Mr Bedford, & Sam Smith.

Mr Oglethorpe reported from the Committee appointed for ⟨that Purpose⟩ Soliciting a Charter at a Meeting on the fourteenth Day of January 1730/1, that pursuant to the Desire of the Trustees they had obtain'd his Majesty's Charter of Incorporation & Grant of Lands to the Trustees for Establishing the Colony of Georgia ⟨in South Carolina⟩ in America, and deliver'd the same

The Thanks of the Trustees were given to Mr Oglethorpe, & the other Gentlemen of the Committee, for the great Care & Trouble they had taken, in soliciting & obtaining the Grant of the said Charter

Mr Oglethorpe reported, that he had receiv'd Proposals from several Persons for making a Common Seal, one ask'd an hundred Pounds, another sixty, another thirty, and another eight, and Mr Oglethorpe was desir'd to agree for that of eight

Mr Oglethorpe was desir'd to draw up a proper Summons, and transmit the same to the Right Hon. the Lord Viscount Percival, his Lordship being oblig'd, pursuant to a certain Clause in the Charter, as President, to appoint a Time & Place of Meeting, & to cause Summonses to be issu'd to the several Members for that Purpose, within thirty Days after their Incorporation

A Letter was read from the Rev. Dr Mawson Vice-Chancellor of Cambridge, wherein he acknowledg'd the Receipt of fourscore of Erasmus his Preacher, & acquainted the Trustees, that he had made a proper Distribution of them in the several Colleges of that University

[*Percival, June 29, 1732*]

... in the evening met as usual the trustees of the Georgia Colony, where Mr. Oglethorp brought us the charter, which was signed the 9th inst., but did not pass all the offices till this week.

. . . .

The charter fees came to 160*l.*, though the Duke of Newcastle forgave his own.

Mr. Pury, a foreigner, came before us. He has obtained a grant of lands, part of South Carolina, on the opposite side of the river Savannah, which bounds our province on the north, and is lately come with some persons of Berne, in Switzerland, to settle a colony there. He has four with him in London, seventy-eight waiting at Calais, and expects a hundred more from Berne.[147]

[*Percival, July 3, 1732*]

I went to town. My principal errand was to take the oath of office as President of the Colony of Georgia; but I learned that some mistakes happening in transcribing the charter, it is necessary they should be amended, and the seal put to it anew. I dsired the charter when amended might be sent to my house on Thursday next.[148]

[*Percival, July 7, 1732*]

Went early in the morning and took my oath of office before the Lord Chief Baron Reynolds at his house in Red Lion Square.[149]

At a Meeting of the Trustees in Palace Court on Thursday July 6 Mr Oglethorpe in the Chair, there being present the Right Hon. the Lord Percival Mr Vernon Mr Holland Mr Hucks Mr Belitha Mr Hales Mr Coram & Sam Smith.

Agreed by the Trustees, that Mr Anderson be desir'd to give them his Assistance in putting their first Books into Order, & that Sam Smith do acquaint him therewith.

Mr Oglethorpe reported from the Right Hon. the Lord Carteret, that his Lordship will concur with the Charter his Majesty has granted to the Trustees, by conveying to them his undivided eighth Part of the Lands in Georgia in such Manner as Mr Attorney General shall advise

Agreed, that Mr Oglethorpe & Mr Holland be desir'd to consult Mr Attorney General thereupon

Mr Oglethorpe lay'd before the Trustees a Form of Summons, which was approv'd of, & deliver'd to the Right Hon. the Lord Percival

Mr Oglethorpe pay'd to ⟨Mr⟩ Richard Atherton the Messenger one Month's Wages at the Rate of two Shillings & six Pence a Week

[*Percival, July 13, 1732*]

... in the evening I met the trustees of the Georgia Settlement.[150]

POSTSCRIPT

It has seemed unnecessary to reproduce the Georgia Charter, for it is easily available in *The Colonial Records of the State of Georgia*, ed. Allen Daniel Candler, Lucian Lamar Knight, Kenneth Coleman, and Milton Ready, 32 vols. to date (Atlanta and Athens, 1904-), 1:11-26; and in Albert Saye's edition—*Georgia's Charter of 1732* (Athens, Ga., 1942). The Minutes of the Bray Associates continue, now in the hand of Benjamin Martyn, until December 3, 1735; but after the Georgia Trustees became legally incorporated, the Bray Associates rarely dealt with the affairs of the Georgia region. The few exceptions follow.

On Monday July 2, 1733, Adam Anderson reported receiving £113/6/10 from the Georgia Trustees—the balance due the Associates. At the same meeting it was ordered that "a Library shall be sent to Georgia for the Use of the Minister in the Town of Savanah as soon as the Trustees hear of the Reverend Mr Quincey's Arrival and Settlement." It was also agreed that "the People in the next Embarkation be furnish'd with Bibles and Common Prayer Books, and other Books for the Use of Families."

On Monday November 4, 1734, "Mr. Verelst acquainted the Associates that he had sent to the Care of Mr. Causton in Savanah in Georgia three Parcels of Books containing in each 3 Bibles, 30 Primmers, 30 small Spelling Books, 30 Horn Books, 20 Testaments & 30 Psalters Directed to Mrs. Hague, Mrs. Drayton & Mr. Bryan,[151] at Charles Town in South Carolina for the Instruction of their Negroes, for him to send by the first Opportunity."

POSTSCRIPT

On Wednesday September 3, 1735, with Percival in the chair and Oglethorpe attending, it was resolved that "a Salary be appointed to a Person for Instructing the Negroes in Purysburgh. Resolved That Thirty Pound a year during Pleasure be the said Salary And That Mr. Oglethorpe be desired to Inquire for a proper Person & the best manner of settling him at Purysburgh for giving such Instructions to the Negroes."

APPENDIX

The persistent suggestions that Captain Thomas Coram or Dr. Thomas Bray was the first to conceive of the Georgia colony originated in the colonial period but owe their currency principally to Professors Albert Saye and Verner W. Crane.

In *The Castle-Builders; or, The History of William Stephens* (1759), the resentful Thomas Stephens noted the resignation as Georgia Trustees of "Mr. *Sloper*, and Mr. *Coram*, who first projected the Colony."[1] But Thomas Stephens was hardly a credible authority: he had no firsthand knowledge of the Georgia genesis; and in his book he was concerned primarily with justifying the actions of his father, the Trustees' secretary and representative in Georgia, who was appointed several years after the colony was founded. The son accused Oglethorpe of "frustrating the Intention of employing Mr. *Stephens* to good Purpose" and of keeping him "*down.*"[2]

In 1940, Albert B. Saye gave new life to the myth. He may have been actuated partly by Arthur Percival Newton's reference in 1937 to "the project of General Oglethorpe and Thomas Coram for the relief of London and other cities from their vagabonds and destitute beggars by their shipment to a new colony to be founded to the south of Carolina."[3] Exaggerating Captain Coram's contribution perhaps in his effort to minimize the importance of Dr. Bray and other clergymen in the Georgia genesis, Saye called one of the captain's petitions for a colony of Georgeia between Maine and Nova Scotia "the skeleton of the Georgia Charter" and suggested that "since Coram was among the first chosen by Oglethorpe to aid in the execution of his project, it is not improbable that Oglethorpe made use of Coram's Nova Scotia scheme in planning the organization for his colony in the southern region."[4] Among more recent historians perhaps Coram's most vigorous advocate has been Paul S. Taylor. In 1972 he named Coram the first "planner" of the colony and commented, "Oglethorpe, for all his distinguished leadership, was not the only planner of Georgia, nor even the first in point of time."[5]

But Coram was chosen not by Oglethorpe, but by the captain's minister, Dr. Bray; and Georgeia was intended for a quite different breed of settlers. Its colonists were originally to be disbanded officers and soldiers, who were noticeably absent from Oglethorpe's Georgia. Late petitions from Coram and his group added New England Irish and French Protestants, who were also absent from Georgia, though the Georgia Trustees would have welcomed the Huguenots. In comparing the associates' plans with Captain Coram's, I can discern few similarities.

The earliest known attribution of the Georgia idea to Dr. Bray comes in a letter that Captain Coram wrote, on April 30, 1734, to the Reverend Benjamin Coleman, in Boston:

> Dr. Bray . . . often Lamented the great pains I for many years took for having a proper Settlement made on the Lands Lying Wast and Derelict between New England and Nova Scotia, told me a little before Christmas 1729 his Death he found drew near for he was sure by his continued decay he should not live out the Winter yet he would before he dyed find out a way to have a Settlement made for the Releife of such honest poor Distressed Famelies from hence as by Losses, want of Employment or otherwise are reduced to poverty and such who were persecuted for their professing the protestant Religion abroad, to be happy by their Labour and Industry in some part of His Majesties Dominions in America but was of Opinion the place I proposed was too far Northward, the Winters being very long there; he sent for

APPENDIX

Mr. James Vernon, the Reverend Dr. Hales, Ld. Percival and Mr. Oglethorpe and 2 or 3 more and proposed their Entering into an association with him tho Confined to his Chamber for the Carrying on his Design of a Colony, and two Designs of his own viz't for Instructing the Negroes in the British Plantations in the Christian Religion; . . . for settling Parochial Libraries in Great Britain; and for other Good purposes; he sent for proper persons to Draw up an instrument suitable to the occations.[6]

The account is at best ambiguous. "His chamber" is obviously Dr. Bray's, but "his Design" must be Oglethorpe's, for Bray's well-known charities are not "his," but "his own." Moreover, the account is clearly biased, coming as it does from Dr. Bray's parishioner and Oglethorpe's most outspoken critic among the Georgia Trustees. Only a month earlier Coram had apparently lodged with the Board of Trade an attack on Oglethorpe's policies in Georgia.[7] It is also inaccurate, as Crane himself demonstrates.[8]

In four studies of Georgia's origin, which he began before Percival's *Diary* and the Bray minutes were made available, Crane added three additional pieces of evidence for Dr. Bray's priority: Dr. Bray's "artisan-mission colonies," advocated in *Missionalia* (1727, 1728); "a persistent tradition among the friends of Bray and the executors of his pious plans that it was Bray who first moved to organize the project of a debtor colony in America"; and Bray's feoffment.

But Dr. Bray's "artisan-mission colonies on the frontiers," "to Christianize and . . . civilize the natives,"[9] were merely small groups of two or three missionary couples, living isolated among the Indians. Evidently recognizing the speciousness of this evidence, in 1962 Crane dropped the suggestion altogether.

As for Dr. Crane's "tradition," we must discriminate between the unreliable American version, spread abroad by Captain Coram, and the comparatively reliable English version, based on Bray's

APPENDIX

official biography. In his letters to the Reverend Benjamin Coleman, Coram evidently misled his Boston correspondent into believing that Dr. Bray even wrote the Georgia Charter, for on March 13, 1735, the *Boston Weekly News Letter* published the following note: "Dr. *Coleman* also thinks it but grateful and just to the Memory of that *Venerable Man of GOD*, Dr. *Bray;* to inform such as knew it not, That He was the *Father* of *three* the most noble and grand *Projections of Piety and Charity* that this last Age, or indeed Ages past have produced. . . . The *third* is the late *Charter* for Incorporating a Number of Gentlemen by the Name of the *Trustees* for Establishing the Colony of *Georgia.* This last the *Doctor* finish'd with his aged *dying* Hand."[10] This American version of the tradition was not confined to the newspapers. In 1749 Ebenezer Turell incorporated the entire quotation in his biography of Dr. Coleman.[11] Dr. Bray died on February 15, 1730; James Vernon presented his first draft of the Georgia Charter to the Bray Associates at their meeting of July 30. Perhaps Captain Coram led Dr. Coleman to confuse the Georgia Charter with Dr. Bray's feoffment, though that document appears not to be in his hand.

In contrast, the British tradition was based on a biography written by Dr. Bray's assistant, the Reverend Mr. Samuel Smith, a Bray Associate. He read it, in Oglethorpe's absence, on June 17, 1730, before four revisers: James Vernon, Rogers Holland, the Reverend Dr. Stephen Hales, and Captain Coram. What revisions the captain suggested then and later we do not know, but he was certainly in a position to make them: when Mr. Smith finally published his biography, in 1746, the captain had been living in his home for a decade:[12]

The Inquiry into the State of the the Gaols, was an event which at this juncture appeared to have something providential, as it gave occasion to an interview between the *doctor* and *Mr Oglethorpe.* This worthy Gentleman, when it was proposd, wanted no arguments to prevail upon him to accept the Trust,

APPENDIX

and engaged several others, some of the first rank and distinction, to act with Him and the former Associates in it.... For to these two Designs of founding Libraries, and instructing the Negroes, a third was now added, which tho' at first view appears to be of a different nature, has a perfect coincidence with them.... a design was form'd of establishing a Colony in *America*. ... ... as the doctor was concerned in getting this undertaking on foot, I can't justly be charged with a digression for taking notice of it.[13]

Thus in spite of whatever pressures Captain Coram may have brought on him, Mr. Smith agreed with Percival that Dr. Bray's involvement with a charitable colony began when he first met with Oglethorpe on the question and offered him charge of the Bray Associates; and Mr. Smith even apologized for mentioning Dr. Bray's role. Captain Coram placed this meeting around Christmas of 1729, when, as Percival makes clear, Oglethorpe had been working at his plan for a debtor colony for the better part of a year.

As for the "continuing tradition" that Crane cited in Edward Bentham's *De Vita et Moribus Johannis Burtoni* (1771) and its review in the *Gentleman's Magazine*, there is nothing in either to support such a "tradition," and in 1962 Crane finally relegated this tradition to a footnote as "of uncertain authority."[14]

Even more important, not a word concerning colonies appears among the charitable projects that Bray championed in 1728 in his *Memorial concerning the Erecting in the City of London or the Suburbs thereof, an Orphanotrophy or Hospital for the Reception of Poor Cast-off Children or Foundlings*, a now-rare pamphlet ascribed to Dr. Bray by Captain Coram and ignored by Bray's biographers.[15]

In 1728, then, Thomas Bray apparently had no concern in colonizing efforts, and his charitable activities were concentrated on his orphanotrophy and the White Chapel and Borough Compter prisons; and even these last were, because of his infirmity, served by surrogates. Oglethorpe's prison investigations were limited to the Fleet, the Marshalsea, and the King's Bench. Thus their prison ministrations probably never brought the two together—until Oglethorpe developed a plan to provide for the released debtors and needed the assistance of Dr. Bray to furnish a legal organization toward that end.

If Dr. Bray had begun to plan a charitable colony before Oglethorpe came to him, Bray's own assistant did not know of it, and neither did his associates. When on February 13, 1730, Oglethorpe explained his Georgia plan to Percival, who was a Bray Associate, the viscount recorded hearing "a Scheme he had form'd, to which I was before a perfect Stranger." On December 28 of that same year, Percival wrote to William Byrd II, of Westover, that "Mr. Oglethorpe a young gentleman of very publick spirit . . . gave the first hint of this project last year, and has very diligently purused it."[16]

Crane's final evidence for Bray's involvement in the Georgia enterprise, however, is accurate.[17] On January 15, 1730, Bray did indeed provide a feoffment intended to enable the dormant Bray Associates to take on new members and a new head; and he arranged to have the new feoffment signed by all the original associates except Percival. Moreover, Bray may have indirectly indicated to Oglethorpe the very means by which he might begin to finance his new colony. For in his *Memorial*, Bray suggested the Joseph King bequest of more than fourteen thousand pounds as a source for charitable projects.[18]

Although Crane was always careful to qualify his suggestions about Bray's alleged priority, some of his followers have not been, though they have advanced no fresh evidence. In 1954 H. P. Thompson, following Samuel Clyde McCullough,[19] implied that Dr. Bray originated the idea of the charitable colony and earlier led Oglethorpe to his prison investigations. In 1963 Trevor Richard Reese wrote, "There is some doubt as to who first proposed the idea" of a charitable colony. "Thomas Coram attributed it to Dr. Thomas Bray, an Anglican clergyman." "For strong argu-

APPENDIX

ment in support of this view see V. W. Crane, *The Southern Frontier*."[20] In 1966 Marion Eugene Sirmans, citing Crane, maintained that "Dr. Bray . . . conceived the idea of a colony for debtors in America."[21] In 1976 Kenneth Coleman was also inclined to credit Dr. Bray: "In 1730, before his prison investigations had been completed, Oglethorpe became concerned about the welfare of the released debtors and began considering a charity colony in America. . . . Dr. Bray seems to have first suggested such a colony shortly before his death in early 1730, and he undoubtedly influenced Oglethorpe's thinking."[22] In his dissertaion " 'Pious Designs' " and his subsequent *Religious Philanthropy and Colonial Slavery* (1985), however, John C. Van Horne was unwilling to credit Dr. Bray with such influence. Although he quoted Coram's claim for Bray and stated that the doctor and Oglethorpe "fortuitously came together" (whatever that means), he admitted that Oglethorpe was forced "to seek out a charitable organization that would be willing to take on the added responsibility of establishing a colony."[23]

NOTES

INTRODUCTION

1. Albert B. Saye, "The Genesis of Georgia: Merchants as well as Ministers," *Georgia Historical Quarterly* (hereafter cited as *GHQ*) 24 (1940): 191-206; *New Viewpoints in Georgia History* (Athens, Ga., 1943), 3-50; "Introductory Statement," *Georgia's Charter of 1732*, ed. Saye (Athens, Ga., 1942), 1-16; "The Genesis of Georgia Reviewed," *GHQ* 50 (1966): 153-61; Verner W. Crane, "The Philanthropists and the Genesis of Georgia," *American Historical Review* 27 (1921): 63-69; *The Southern Frontier, 1670-1732*, with preface by Peter H. Wood (New York, 1981), 303-25; "The Origins of Georgia," *GHQ* 14 (1930): 93-110; "Dr. Thomas Bray and the Charitable Colony Project," *William and Mary Quarterly* (hereafter cited as *WMQ*), 3d series, 19 (1962): 49-63. See also Geraldine Meroney, "The London Entrepôt Merchants and the Georgia Colony," *WMQ*, 3d series, 15 (1968): 230-44.

2. John Viscount Percival, *Diary of Viscount Percival, Afterwards First Earl of Egmont*, ed. R. A. Roberts, Historical Manuscripts Commission, 3 vols. (London, 1920-23), 1:45.

3. Percival, *Diary*, 1:45.

4. See John C. Van Horne, "'Pious Designs': The American Correspondence of the Associates of Dr. Bray, 1731-1775," a University of Virginia dissertation (1979), 1:11-40; and *Religious Philanthropy and Colonial Slavery: The American Correspondence of the Associates of Dr. Bray, 1717-1777* (Urbana and Chicago: University of Illinois Press, 1985), 4-16.

5. See D. G. C. Allan and R. E. Schofield, *Stephen Hales: Scientist and Philanthropist* (London, 1980), 4, 67, 143.

6. The Reverend Richard King, vicar of Topsham in Devonshire, and the Reverend Digby Cotes, principal of Magdalen College, Oxford, and public orator of the university, were too busy or too distant to act. Neither the elderly Thomas Carpenter of Friday St. nor Mr. "Smith of the Temple, Esq.," both evidently trustees of the Joseph King bequest, accepted. Nor did Oliver St. John, Esq., of Lincoln's Inn, who was apparently abroad. Henry Hastings, Esq., sent five pounds but never appeared at a meeting. To these should be added two members of Parliament who were serving on Oglethorpe's prison committee: John Campbell of Calder, Nairne, and Erasmus Phillips, who eventually became a Georgia Trustee in March of 1733.

7. Percival, "Account of Georgia: The Leading Steps to His Maj[est]y's Grant of the Charter," British Library Add. MS 47000, fol. 53. This important account, apparently written on March 2, 1731, has been unfortunately neglected.

8. Since 1932, a minor myth has flourished that originally Oglethorpe intended to establish his first colony in the West Indies. In 1971 Milton Ready suggested that the associates "sought to settle a colony" there ("The Georgia Concept: An Eighteenth Century Experiment in Colonization," *GHQ* 55:163). In 1979 Edward S. Gaustad even located the mythical colony in Bermuda (*George Berkeley in America* [New Haven, 1979], 101). But from Percival's "Account of Georgia," it is clear that the initial location chosen was "on the Continent." Crane in 1921 and again in 1928 and Saye in 1943 clarified Percival's ambiguous "West Indies," and Saye explained that "Percival frequently used the term 'West Indies' for America" (*New Viewpoints*, 17, n. 33). Of the thirteen appearances of the term "West Indies" in Percival's *Diary*, only one refers exclusively to these islands. Three references, on the other hand, refer principally or exclusively to the seaboard colonies, including New England. Percival's usage was typical: for example, discus-

sions of the seaboard colonies, including New England, were all placed under the rubric of "West Indies" in the *Historical Register* for 1729-31. The context of Percival's reference, especially the crops expected and the enemies feared, also clearly place the intended colony on the mainland.

9. "An act for the relief of insolvent debtors," 2 George II, cap. 20, Great Britain, Parliament. *The Statutes at Large*, ed. Danby Pickering, 46 vols. (Cambridge, 1762-1807), 16:44-45.

10. Percival, *Diary*, 1:44-46.

11. Percival, *Diary*, 1:93.

12. Percival, "Account of Georgia," fol. 55 recto. There the event is apparently dated July 1; but in the *Diary*, July 31.

13. R. A. Roberts, "The Birth of an American State: Georgia: An Effort of Philanthropy and Protestant Propaganda," *Transactions of the Royal Historical Society*, 4th series, 6 (1923): 24-25; Amos Aschbach Ettinger, *James Edward Oglethorpe: Imperial Idealist* (Oxford, 1936; rpt., Archon, 1968), 111, 122.

14. Georgia, *The Colonial Records of Georgia*, ed. Allen D. Candler, Lucian Lamar Knight, Kenneth Coleman, and Milton Ready, 32 vols. to date (Atlanta and Athens, 1904-), 1:123.

15. For example, on July 25th, as Percival noted, "Mr. Oglethorp came to dine with me, and discourse the charter we design to apply for" (*Diary*, 1:99).

16. See the introduction to Oglethorpe's *Some Account of the Design of the Trustees for establishing Colonys in America*, ed. Rodney M. Baine and Phinizy Spalding (Athens, Ga., 1990), xxvii-xxviii.

17. On February 5, 1731, Newman wrote Bishop Berkeley, "You will hear of a Project vigorously espous'd by Mr Oglethorpe & several other active members of Parliament . . . for sending a Colony of our poor helpless People from hence . . . under the Direction of Capt Coram." W. O. B. Allen and Edmund McClure, *Two Hundred Years: The History of the Society for Promoting Christian Knowledge* (London, 1898; rpt., Franklin, 1970), 247.

18. Rodney M. Baine and Mary E. Williams, "Oglethorpe's

Early Military Campaigns," *Yale University Library Gazette* 60 (1985): 63-76.

19. Percival, *Diary*, 1:219.

20. Anonymous and untitled, this appeal appeared in the *London Journal* on July 29, 1732. In my forthcoming edition of *The Published Works of James Edward Oglethorpe*, I entitle it "An Appeal for the Georgia Colony."

BRAY MINUTES, 1730-1732,
AND SUPPLEMENTARY DOCUMENTS

1. Peter King (1669-1734), first baron King, of Ockham, Speaker of the House of Lords.

2. Arthur Onslow (1691-1768), of Imber Court, Surrey.

3. Percival, *Diary*, 1:44-46.

4. The Bray feoffment, from a photostat in the Hargrett Rare Book and Manuscript Library of the University of Georgia. The original, a single sheet, was never legally executed and is now in the archives of the United Society for the Propagation of the Gospel. Chiefly to avoid some of the repetition, I have made a number of cuts, indicated by spaced suspension points. The infrequent minuscule additions made in superscript, chiefly to show locations, I have omitted, as they appear to have been added later and in a different hand. The feoffment appears in its entirety in John C. Van Horne's *Religious Philanthropy and Colonial Slavery*, 62-67.

5. So far the Reverend Mr. Arthur Bedford's title page; a later hand added "according to Mr D'Allone's Charity from March 21st 1729, to Decr. 3d. 1735." I have not reproduced Bedford's head title, which omits the last "for" of his title page.

6. Percival, *Diary*, 1:90.

7. Percival, *Diary*, 1:93.

8. Both this list and the clause in item 2 beginning "and they signified" actually appear on the previous page, which is otherwise blank. They are positioned here at the suggestion of Alan S.

Bell, Esq., of the Rhodes House Library. Bedford's asterisks indicate placement.

9. *To the Honourable and Worthy Gentlemen, the Trustees of Mr. D'Allone's Bequest for converting the Negroes.* Some copies were bound up with Bray's *Missionalia* (London, 1726, 1727). See Samuel C. McCullough, "Thomas Bray's *Missionalia*," the *Historical Magazine of the Protestant Episcopal Church* 15 (1946): 232–45.

10. One convenience of having numerous members of Parliament among the associates was utilizing their privilege of franking.

11. The Reverend Edmund Gibson (1669–1748) had been bishop of London since 1720.

12. This is the first recorded mention of the location for the proposed colony.

13. A generous philanthropist, the Lady Elizabeth Hastings (1682–1739) was the daughter of Theophilus, seventh earl of Huntingdon. Her head was engraved on the reverse of the medal struck in 1735 in honor of General Oglethorpe.

14. Percival, *Diary*, 1:98.

15. The minutes for this meeting were twice recorded. The first version was corrected and signed by Oglethorpe; the second, a clean transcript, was also approved by him. The first version, which omits the list of members present, begins, "Mr Oglethorpe rep[orte]d Twenty ⟨Guineas⟩ Pounds being paid to the Trustees by a Person unknown, to be applied to the Charitable Colony ⟨by the Hands of Mr Oglethorpe⟩ and five Guineas ⟨by⟩ Mr Belitha by the Hands of the Rd Mr Hales, agreed, that it be kept by Mr Oglethorpe until farther Orders."

16. Ordained by the bishop of London in 1730, the Reverend Mr. Fulton was sent to Christ Church, in South Carolina. He was apparently discharged in 1734 because of neglected duties or unsatisfactory conduct.

17. Except where the left margin is torn, x's there accompany each check mark, and one also occurs opposite Oglethorpe's name.

18. In the left margin was later added the word "abroad."

19. "Mr. Gardiner," a member of the SPCK, was apparently the Reverend Mr. James Gardiner (d. 1732), son of the bishop of Lincoln. Henry Newman (1670–1743) became secretary of the SPCK in 1708, with headquarters at Bartlett's Buildings. Born in Rehobath, Massachusetts, he graduated from Harvard with an A.B. in 1687 and an M.A. in 1690. The Reverend Francis Fox became chaplain to the Lord Mayor of London in 1705 and vicar of St. Mary, Reading, in 1726. He published an edition of the New Testament and *An Introduction to Spelling and Reading, containing Lessons for Children.*

20. Phillips's name is crossed out here and earlier, in the main list, but it is not clear when it was deleted.

21. "An act for the better preservation of parochial libraries," 7 Anne, cap. 14; Pickering's *Statutes*, 11:492.

22. Probably the Reverend John Price, rector of Newton Tony, Wiltshire, who in 1730 published a sermon for the relief of the German and French Protestants at Copenhagen, or the Reverend Mr. Samuel Price, who in 1725 preached before Bray's Society for the Reformation of Manners.

23. Baron Augustus Schutz was the ambassador to England from Hanover. The Prince of Wales was Frederick Louis, who died in 1751.

24. Built by the Swedes in 1655 and seized by the British in 1663 from the Portuguese, Cape Coast Castle, in the center of the seaboard of present Ghana, was the administrative capital of the Gold Coast. In 1720 the Royal African Company requested the SPG to recommend chaplains, guaranteeing eighty pounds or one hundred pounds yearly and keep, but the first missionary or chaplain sent there arrived in 1751.

25. This minute of thanks is not in Bedford's hand.

26. David Humphreys, secretary of the SPG, published in 1730 *An Historical account of the Incorporated Society for the Propagation of the Gospel in Foreign Parts.*

27. Percival, *Diary*, 1:99. Sir Nathaniel Mead, sergeant at law, was an M.P. from 1715 until 1722.

28. Great Britain, Privy Council, *Acts of the Privy Council of England. Colonial Series*, 6 vols., ed. Sir Almeric W. Fitzroy, W. L. Grant, and James Munro (London, 1908-12), 3:299 (hereinafter cited as *APC*).

29. Presumably the Reverend Thomas Frank the younger (1699-1784), who became rector of Cranfield, Bedfordshire, in 1731. His father, then rector there, corresponded with the SPCK extensively in 1700. A small parish and village, Streatley is four and a half miles north of Lupton.

30. Howe, also a tiny parish and village, is six and a half miles northeast of Norfolk.

31. The Reverend Joseph Holt, a graduate of Jesus College, Cambridge, was temporary minister at Poplar Spring, Gloucester County, Virginia, from 1697 until 1700. Leaving Virginia because of his scandalous behavior, he then went to Maryland, and in 1711, to Barbados, as first minister to the Codrington estate and college there. Here again his scandalous behavior led to his discharge, in 1714.

32. In Jamaica slaves had long been escaping to the mountains and forming villages there, especially during the period 1728-38. The militia and even regiments occasionally sent from Britain were unable to suppress them. Disappointed in securing a commission in Georgia, Philip Thicknesse received an appointment in such a regiment. But the associates were misinformed about Virginia. In 1729 a large body of blacks belonging to a plantation in the upper reaches of the James River fled, with arms and farming implements, to the Blue Ridge Mountains. They were overpowered by their pursuers. In 1730 some two hundred slaves from Norfolk and Princess Anne counties, while the whites were at church, met to revolt. Four were executed. The *Virginia Gazette* later reported that some of the slaves had heard that the king had ordered free-

dom for those who became Christian. Governor Gooch ordered that every white man must bring his arms to church on Sundays and holidays.

33. The elderly H. Hatley had been a stationer and bookseller since 1682.

34. Barnaby Bernard Lintot was the respected publisher of Pope's *Iliad* and *Odyssey*. He had been in business in London from 1698.

35. Bernard Lamy, *Apparatus Biblicus; or, An Introduction to the Scriptures*, 2d ed., 2 vols. (London, 1728). Mrs. Martin was Dr. Bray's daughter Tabitha.

36. Desiderius Erasmus, *Des. Erasmi . . . Ecclesiastes, Liber primus*, ed. Bray (London, 1730).

37. From almost the beginning of her reign, Queen Anne saw to it that Parliament provided funds to augment the livings of the poorer clergy. See John Ecton, *A State of the Proceedings of the Corporation of the Governors of the Bounty of Queen Anne*, 2d ed. (London, 1721).

38. James Blair (president of William and Mary), *Our Saviours Divine Sermon on the Mount*, 5 vols. (London, 1722, 1723). Apparently the associates had been given the copyright.

39. Great Britain, Public Record Office, Colonial Office, 5/362: fols. 2-3, from the ACLS microfilm (hereinafter cited by CO number only). It is entered on fol. 5v, "South Carolina Order of Committee of the 23d. Novr: last, referring to the Board a Petn. from Ld. Percival and sevl: others praying for a Charter of Incorporation for settling poor People in S. Carolina where they pray for Land for this Purpose. Recd / Read Decr: 3d: 1730." It is docketed "D:2." See also Great Britain, Public Record Office, *Calendar of State Papers, Colonial Series. America and West Indies*, 44 vols. to date, ed. W. Noël Sainbury et al. (London, 1860-), 37:357-58 (hereinafter cited as *CSP*). A transcription appears in *Records in the British Public Record Office relating to South Carolina, 1663-1782*, transcriptions microfilmed by William McDowell, vols. 6-36, in

six reels (Columbia, South Carolina, 1955), reel 2, 14:285-88 (hereafter cited as *Records*). Brief is *APC*, 3:299-300.

40. Governor Robert Johnson was probably responding to a letter from Oglethorpe.

41. *Records*, 14:25-26. See also Great Britain, Public Record Office, *Journal of the Commissioners for Trade and Plantations*, ed. H. C. Maxwell Lyte, A. E. Stamp, K. H. Ledward et al., 14 vols. (London, 1920-38), 4:165 (hereinafter cited as *JCTP*), which identifies the members present as the earl of Westmoreland, Mr. Pelham, Mr. Bladen, and Sir A. Croft: Thomas Fane, sixth earl of Westmoreland, Lord Le Despenser; Thomas Pelham, of Lewes (1678-1760); Colonel Martin Bladen (1680-1746), a member of Oglethorpe's prison committee and a longtime member of the board; and Sir Archer Croft (1683-1753), second baronet Croft of Croft Castle, Herefordshire, appointed in 1730. Sir John Gonson (d. 1765) was the popular chairman of the Westminster quarter sessions. He became a Georgia Trustee on March 13, 1733.

42. CO 5/362: fols. 7-9. On fol. 10r, Oglethorpe's cover letter (which appears to be in his own hand) is addressed "To Popple, Esq. These." The documents are entered on fol. 10v as "South Carolina, Lr from Mr Oglethorpe of the 7th Decemr 1730 with Proposals from the Petitioners for Establishing a Charitable Colony in South Carolina Recd 7: / Read 9th Decr: 1730." They are docketed "D:3." See also *CSP*, 37:383-84, and *Records*, 14:289-91. Several generations of Popples served as secretaries to the Board of Trade; the one then serving was Alured Popple.

43. Sir John Brownlow, Viscount Tyrconnel (1690-1754), was a member of Oglethorpe's second prison committee. He became a Georgia Trustee on March 15, 1733. Archibald Hutchinson (c. 1659-1740), was an M.P. from 1713 until 1727. Sir William Chapman, Lord Mayor of London, was a wealthy director of the South Sea Company. Sir Joseph Eyles, a Turkey merchant, was M.P. for Southwark.

44. *Records*, 14:26-27. *JCTP*, 6:167-68, lists the board mem-

bers present as the earl of Westmoreland, Mr. Docminique, Mr. Pelham, and Mr. Bladen. Paul Docminique, of Clipstead, Surrey (1643-1735) had been a member of the board since 1714.

45. There follow a ruled line and, in a later hand, the comment "So far as the black Line referr'd to further Consideration."

46. *Records*, 14:27-28. *JCTP*, 6:169, lists as present Mr. Dominique, Mr. Pelham, Mr. Bladen, and Sir A. Croft; and it adds after "disapproved of by him" the phrase "in . . . days," annotating it *"Left blank in original."*

47. *Records*, 14:28. See also *JCTP*, 6:170.

48. CO 5/401: pp. 8-14, a fair copy. In the left margin of page 8 it is entered as "Rept. to the Lords of the Committee of Council upon the Petition of the Lord Percival; Edrd. Digby, Geo: Carpenter Esq &ca. about Establishing a Charitable Colony in S Carolina." See also *Records*, 14:294-300; and *CSP*, 37:394-97. The laws 7 & 8 William III, cap. 22, especially sec. 16, and 12 Charles II, cap. 18, especially sec. 2, provided that all colonial governors must take oaths to enforce the provisions of the present act and previous acts governing colonial trade. See "An act for preventing frauds, and regulating abuses in the plantation trade" (Pickering's *Statutes*, 9:428-36) and "An act for the encouraging and increasing of shipping and navigation" (*Statutes*, 7:452-60).

49. CO 5/362: fols. 11-12. It was entered on fol. 17v as "South Carolina. Order of the Committee of Council of the 12th: Janry 1730 referring back to the Board of Trade a Paragraph of their late Report upon the Petition of the Ld. V. Percival & others, relating to the Establishmt. of a Charitable Colony in South Carolina, to consider of some Alteration proposed therein Recd / Read Janry 13th: 1730/1." It was docketed "D:4." See also *Records*, reel 3, 15:6-7; *CSP*, 38:3-4; and *APC*, 3:300. Temple Stanyan (d. 1752) replaced his older brother Abraham as clerk for the Privy Council in 1719.

50. *Records*, 15:1. See also *JCTP*, 4:175. Present were Mr. Docminique, Mr. Pelham, Mr. Bladen, Mr. Brudenell, and Sir A. Croft. James Brudenell (c. 1687-1746) was appointed in 1730.

51. *Records*, 15:1. See also *JCTP*, 4:175. Present were the same members as on the previous day.

52. CO 5/381: fols. 79-80, from the microfilm in *Miscellaneous Papers and Letters concerning South Carolina, app. 1722-1774*, 2 reels, reel 1. It was entered on fol. 8ov as "South Carolina Report to the Lords of the Committee of Council, relating to some Alterations proposed to be made in a late Report of the Board by the Petrs. for a Charitable Colony in South Carolina   Janry 14th: 1730/1." It was docketed "Ent: B. Folio—15." A fair copy is CO 5/401: p. 15. See also *Records*, 15:8-9, and *CSP*, 38:12-13. Sir Orlando Bridgeman, the second baronet (1679-1746), supported the Bray Associates in the Board of Trade and in Parliament.

53. Perhaps John Disney's short *View of Ancient Laws against Immorality and Profaneness . . . Perjury* (Cambridge, 1729).

54. John Edwards, *Veritax Redux . . . a Compleat Body of Divinity*, 3 vols. (London, 1707, 1708, 1725-26).

55. Not a bookseller, James Martin was the husband of Dr. Bray's daughter Tabitha.

56. Following this paragraph, the secretary wrote the following subject headings in the left margin: "Erasmus Cambridge / Oxford / King's Legacy."

57. The Reverend Thomas Randolph (1701-83), who was at Corpus Christi, Oxford, during Oglethorpe's last year there, was to become president of the college and vice chancellor of the university.

58. Probably Burton's *Heli* and his *Hapni & Phinees* (Oxford, 1729).

59. CO 5/362: fols. 26-30r. It is entered on fol. 31v as "South Carolina. Copy of an Order in Council, of 28th. Janry. 1730-1, directing the Attorney & Solicitor Genl. to prepare the Draught of a Charter, upon the Petition of the Ld. Visct. Percival & others, praying for a Grant of Land in South Carolina, to settle poor Families there. Recd. 10th. / Read 11th. Augst. 1731." It is docketed "D:9. "See also *Records*, 15:10-15; *CSP*, 38:29; and *APC*, 3:300-303.

60. Percival, *Diary*, 1:127.

61. Oglethorpe alludes to the act 9 Anne cap. 21, section 42; Pickering's *Statutes*, 12:219.

62. Percival, *Diary*, 1:128–29.

63. In the left margin of these minutes, the secretary recorded the following headings: "Books lettered / Bind Clarkes Treatises / Who to write the / Names of Parishes / in Paroch. / Libraries. / Binding Register Books. / Printing Rules for / Preserving Libraries. / 4tos to be bought. / Mr Smiths Proposals, / 6 Erasmus Ecc. / to Mr. Dobbs. / 1 to each Irish Bishops, / ? whether the Lord / Percival would / undertake the / sending them."

64. The Reverend Richard Dobbs, a relative of Arthur Dobbs, governor of North Carolina from 1754 to 1765.

65. Although this action is scored out, it is not bracketed here because it is preceded by the note "not d."

66. In the left-hand margin of this action are the heads: "Mr Burton's / Library. / Libraries. / How. / Collerne. / Stretly."

67. John Carteret, first earl of Granville (1690–1763), was the only proprietor who had not relinquished his rights to the province.

68. Percival, *Diary*, 1:154.

69. Percival, *Diary*, 1:155.

70. Percival, *Diary*, 1:155. The attorney general was Philip Yorke, first earl of Hardwicke (1690–1764).

71. Percival, *Diary*, 1:157.

72. Percival, *Diary*, 1:157.

73. Bethlehem Hospital, founded in 1247, gradually became a hospital devoted entirely to lunatics. Westminster Infirmary was founded in 1715 as a charitable hospital.

74. Percival, *Diary*, 1:157.

75. As Phinizy Spalding has argued in "Some Sermon Preached before the Trustees of Colonial Georgia," *GHQ* 57 (1973): 332–46, the Bray anniversary sermon played a part in the promotional campaign.

76. A bookseller and publisher, Thomas Page (d. 1733) followed and preceded others of the same name on Tower Hill.

77. Government lotteries authorized by Parliament were held from 1709 until 1824. The ten-pound tickets were ordinarily sold at a premium and were then frequently retailed.

78. Percival, *Diary*, 1:164.

79. Percival, *Diary*, 1:165.

80. Percival, *Diary*, 1:167-68.

81. Executor John Coke's elder brother, Thomas (1674-1727), of Trusley, an M.P. for Derbyshire early in the century, was Vice-Chancellor of the Household from 1706. His daughter Charlotte married Matthew Lambe, the other executor.

82. Percival, *Diary*, 1:172.

83. Dr. Bray's "Lectures" were his popular *Catechetical Lectures*, published in 1696. William Allen's *Discourse on . . . the Two Covenants* appeared in 1673. Allen's third edition of John Kettlewell's *Practical Believer* was published in 1712, 1713. The author was a friend of Dr. Bray.

84. "This book is designed for those who serve in sacred orders, and in Academia."

85. The original minutes of this meeting recorded several actions: the three present obviously expected the arrival of others to constitute a quorum. Later, the minutes were so heavily deleted that I cannot decipher them.

86. Percival, *Diary*, 1:188.

87. The Reverend Mr. Sam Smith recorded the rest of the minutes recorded here, except for those given in the Postscript, which are in the hand of Benjamin Martyn, secretary of the Georgia Trustees and the Bray Associates.

88. The Reverend Samuel Smith's biography of Dr. Bray remained unpublished until it finally appeared, anonymously, in 1746 as *Publick Spirit, Illustrated in the Life and Designs of the Reverend Thomas Bray, D.D.*

89. Percival, *Diary*, 1:193.

90. The Mine Adventure was developed by Sir Humphrey Mackworth to finance mines and smelting works in Wales. Dr. Bray was an early investor. See H. P. Thompson, *Thomas Bray* (London, 1954), 37, 101.

91. *APC*, 3:303.

92. In 1725 Sir William Perkins founded and endowed at Chertsey a school for twenty-five poor boys and twenty-five poor girls.

93. Ms. Aldey may have been one of Dr. Bray's servants, Margaret Harris or Sarah Walker.

94. Adam Anderson's response is in the British Library as Sloane MS 4501, pp. 310-14. See H. P. Thompson, *Thomas Bray* (London, 1954), 110.

95. Percival, *Diary*, 1:204.

96. The Reverend Samuel Netham, or Needham, was probably a relative of the Reverend Joseph Needham, vicar of Colerne, Wiltshire, from 1726 until 1760.

97. The Reverend Charles Wadsworth, son of the Reverend Nathaniel Wadsworth, succeeded his father as rector of Howe in 1729.

98. Probably Charles Bolton, a prosperous Bridgetown, Barbados, merchant then in London, was questioned about the conversion and education of the blacks on Barbados.

99. Head of a banking firm, Sir Francis Child the younger (1684?-1740), M.P. from 1722, was alderman of London in 1722, sheriff in 1722, and Lord Mayor in 1731.

100. Percival, *Diary*, 1:209.

101. CO 5/362: fol. 48. It is entered on fol. 53v as "South Carolina Order from the Committee of Council, dated the 14th. of Decemr: 1731, referring to the Board of Trade some points relating to a Charter for Establishing Colonys in South Carolina or other parts of America. Recd / Read Decem: 17th: 1731." It is docketed "D:15." See also *Records*, 15:65; and *CSP*, 38:369.

102. *APC*, 3:303-5.

103. *Records*, 15:5. See also *JBTP*, 6:259.

104. CO 5/381: fols. 87-88. It is entered on fol. 88v as "So: Carolina Rept. to the Lds. of the Committee of Council, abt. Settling A Western Boundary to the Colony to be Established in South Carolina, by a Charter, for which the Lord Percival & others have petitioned. Decemr: 22d. 1731." It is docketed "Ent. B: Folio. 24." A fair copy is CO 5/401: fols. 23-24. See also *CSP*, 38:390; and *Records*, 15:76-77.

105. The commissary was then the Reverend Mr. Jacob Henderson.

106. *APC*, 3:305.

107. Percival, *Diary*, 1:216-17. Spencer Compton, earl of Wilmington (1673?-1743), a member of the council since 1716, became Lord Privy Seal and President of the council in 1730. Alexander Campbell, second earl of Marchmont (1675-1740), became a member in 1726; Admiral George Byng, Viscount Torrington (1663-1733), in 1721; Sir William Strickland (c.1686-1735), only in 1730; Horatio Walpole, first baron Walpole (1678-1757), son of Robert Walpole, also in 1730; Archibald Campbell, duke of Argyll and viscount of Islay (1682-1761), in 1711. The last was a relative of Oglethorpe; Sir William married a daughter of Oglethorpe's friend Sir Jeremy Sambrook.

108. Percival, *Diary*, 1:217.

109. CO 5/362: fols. 91-92. It is entered on fol. 96v as "South Carolina—Georgia Copy of An Order in Council, of the 27th: of January 1731/2, approving the Draught of a Charter for Establishing a New Colony in His Majesty's Province of South Carolina, by the Name of the Colony of Georgia. Reced 15th: Augt. Read 7th. Sept. 1732." It is docketed "D:29." See also *Records*, 15:95: and *CSP*, 39:32. William Sharpe was secretary to the Privy Council.

110. Percival, *Diary*, 1:219.

111. Percival, *Diary*, 1:220.

112. In the introduction to Oglethorpe's *Some Account of the Design of the Trustees*, I mistakenly identified this regular meeting

with the special meeting, on February 4, of an editorial committee met to consider Oglethorpe's manuscript.

113. Percival, *Diary*, 1:223.

114. John Drummond, of Sterling (1676-1742), probably authored one of the letters printed in the appendix of Oglethorpe's *Sailor's Advocate* (1728).

115. Percival, *Diary*, 1:223-24.

116. As we can see here, the Bray anniversary sermons were at first not well attended, and the first to be printed did not appear until after the associates became the Georgia Trustees. Percival was prevented by his parliamentary duties from attending the first sermon. Brawn's eating house was probably run by Samuel Brawne, the grandfather of Fanny Brawne, the love of John Keats.

117. Percival, *Diary*, 1:225-26.

118. The speaker's chamber was used primarily for committee meetings. Oglethorpe's prison committees frequently met there.

119. Percival, *Diary*, 1:226-27.

120. Percival, *Diary*, 1:230.

121. Percival, *Diary*, 1:231.

122. Percival, *Diary*, 1:231-32.

123. Percival, *Diary*, 1:232.

124. Percival, *Diary*, 1:235.

125. Percival, *Diary*, 1:236. Bishop Berkeley wanted the money to go to Yale College.

126. Percival, *Diary*, 1:240.

127. The page on which the original minutes were made was torn, and the minutes were again recorded by Mr. Smith.

128. Percival, *Diary*, 1:254.

129. The application for the charter was signed by twenty-one associates, and these were listed in the charter. Evidently Percival was thinking of the fifteen members of the Common Council, which transacted the important business.

130. Percival, *Diary*, 1:260-61.

131. Percival, *Diary*, 1:262.

132. Probably the *Primordia Bibliothecaria* (1726).
133. Perhaps Dr. Henry More, the Platonist, *The Theological Works* (London, 1708), published especially for charitable libraries.
134. Percival, *Diary*, 1:264.
135. Percival, *Diary*, 1:265.
136. Percival, *Diary*, 1:266.
137. Percival, *Diary*, 1:272-73.
138. Percival, *Diary*, 1:273-74.
139. Percival, *Diary*, 1:274.
140. Percival, *Diary*, 1:276.
141. Percival, *Diary*, 1:277.
142. Percival, *Diary*, 1:278.
143. Justice Nathaniel Blackerby succeeded Sir John Gonson as chairman of the Westminster Sessions in 1737. Justice Blackerby continued the legal publications of his father, Samuel Blackerby. The house that the associates rented as the Georgia Office was near the Old Palace Yard, just south of Westminster Hall, close to the London residence of Oglethorpe and his mother.
144. Dr. Matthias Mawson (1683-1770) was Master of Benet, or Corpus Christi College, from 1724 until 1744 and chaplain to the king from 1727 until 1739.
145. Robert Elwes, son of Jeremy E. Elwes, of Lincolnshire, studied law at Gray's Inn before succeeding his older brother in the family estate. He died June 10, 1731.
146. Percival, *Diary*, 1:282.
147. Percival, *Diary*, 1:282-83.
148. Percival, *Diary*, 1:283. On April 30, 1730, James Reynolds (1686-1739) became Lord Chief Baron of the Exchequer.
149. Percival, *Diary*, 1:283.
150. Percival, *Diary*, 1:285.
151. As early as 1713, Mrs. Lilia Haig was educating her numerous blacks in the Christian religion. Mrs. Ann Drayton, who assisted in the founding of Savannah and who on June 2, 1736, acknowledged receipt of the books, was married to Thomas Drayton by 1705,

and died in 1742. Her son Thomas married the daughter of Oglethorpe's friend William Bull. Both Jonathan and Hugh Bryan were later devoted disciples of the Reverend George Whitefield. See the interesting discussion of the Bryans' religious activities in Alan Gallay, *The Formation of a Planter Elite* (Athens, Ga., 1989), 30-54.

APPENDIX

1. Thomas Stephens, *The Castle-Builders; or, The History of William Stephens, of the Isle of Wight, Esq.* (London, 1759), 106.
2. Stephens, *The Castle-Builders*, 116, 94.
3. Newton, Introduction, *CSP*, 37:xli.
4. Albert B. Saye, "The Genesis of Georgia: Merchants as well as Ministers," *GHQ* 24 (1940): 193. See also Saye's *New Viewpoints in Georgia History* (Athens, Ga., 1943), 4.
5. Paul S. Taylor, *Georgia Plan, 1732-1752* (Berkeley and Los Angeles, 1972), 19, n. 34.
6. Thomas Coram to the Reverend Benjamin Coleman, April 30, 1734, in Massachusetts Historical Society, *Proceedings*, 56 (1922): 20-21.
7. Ibid., 56:21. There was a meeting of the Board of Trade on the day Coram mentioned (March 27, 1734), but no mention of his protest was recorded in the published record. See *JBTP*, 6:381-82.
8. Crane, "Dr. Thomas Bray and the Charitable Colony Project, 1730," *WMQ*, 3d series, 19 (1962): 62-63.
9. Bernard C. Steiner, "Two Eighteenth Century Missionary Plans," *Sewanee Review* 11 (1903): 302, quoting *Missionalia*.
10. The *Boston Weekly News Letter*, March 13, 1735, p. 4.
11. Ebenezer Turell, *The Life and Character of the late Reverend Dr. Coleman* (Boston, 1749), 145-46, n.
12. H. B. Fant, "Picturesque Thomas Coram," *GHQ* 32 (1948): 97, 101.
13. "A Short Historical Account of Dr. Bray's Life and Designs," in *Rev. Thomas Bray: His Life and Selected Works*, ed. Bernard C.

Steiner, Maryland Historical Society Fund Publication No. 37 (1901; rpt., Arno Press, 1972), 47-48. The final sentence does not appear in the version published in 1746 as *Publick Spirit, Illustrated in the Life and Designs of the Reverend Thomas Bray.* For Smith's authorship of both versions, see Crane, "Philanthropists," 27:63, n. 3.

14. Crane, "Charitable Colony," 14:63, n. 32.

15. *The National Union Catalog: Pre-1956 Imprints* (Chicago, 1968-81), 73:294, citing Coram's inscription on the title page of the copy in the Harvard College Library. It was attributed to Dr. Bray also by H. B. Fant, in "Picturesque Thomas Coram," 32:91.

16. *The Correspondence of the Three William Byrds of Westover, Virginia, 1684-1776,* ed. Marion Tinling, 2 vols. (Charlottesville, Va., 1977), 1:440.

17. Crane, *Southern Frontier,* 318-19; Crane, "Charitable Colony," 19:52-54

18. Bray, *A Memorial concerning the Erecting ... an Orphanotrophy* (London, 1728), 25.

19. Samuel Clyde McCullough, "Dr. Thomas Bray's Final Years at Aldgate," *Historical Magazine of the Protestant Episcopal Church* 14 (1945): 334; H. P. Thompson, *Thomas Bray* (London, 1954), 97-98. In his "Picturesque Thomas Coram" (p. 91), H. B. Fant gave the credit to Dr. Bray, rather than Coram. In his biographical sketch of Dr. Bray in the *DNB*, John Henry Overton credited Oglethorpe with the colonial idea.

20. Trevor Richard Reese, *Colonial Georgia: A Study in British Imperial Policy in the Eighteenth Century* (Athens, Ga., 1963), 9, 138, n. 9.

21. Marion Eugene Sirmans, *Colonial South Carolina: A Political History, 1663-1763* (Chapel Hill, 1966), 169.

22. Kenneth Coleman, *Colonial Georgia: A History* (New York, 1976), 15.

23. John C. Van Horne, *Religious Philanthropy,* 10. See also his "'Pious Designs,'" 29-30.

INDEX

Adderly, John, and family, xxv, 78
Alatamaha River: as a border, 27, 38, 43, 48, 50, 62, 90, 91
Aldey, Mr. and Mrs. Roger, 83, 140 (n. 93)
Allen, William, 78, 139 (n. 83)
Alortamalla River. *See* Alatamaha River
America (British North America), xxii, 71, 125; clergymen and blacks in, 16, 68, 77, 82; blacks revolt in, 28, 31, 133 (n. 32); colonies in, 37, 38, 49, 51, 61, 107, 110, 120; laws for colonies in, 64; books for missionaries in, 76. *See also* Carolina; Georgia; New England; Rhode Island; South Carolina; Virginia
Anderson, Adam, xix, 33, 72, 76, 117; chosen by Oglethorpe, xvi; named in feoffment, 7; attends meetings of associates and Georgia Trustees, 9, 11, 12, 17, 18, 28, 29, 40, 45, 56, 59, 66, 67, 70, 73, 82, 83, 84, 85, 86, 87, 91, 93, 94, 103, 105, 112, 113; address of, 20; helps with records, 22–23, 32, 115, signs petition, 38, 39; to edit Smith's sermon, 75; helps with annuities and stocks, 83, 84, 94; letter to Sloane, 83, 140 (n. 94)
Anderson, Captain, 95
Anne (queen of Great Britain and Ireland), 34, 134 (n. 37)
Anne (first transport to Georgia), xxi
Annesley, Francis, xviii, 11
Argyll, Archibald Campbell, third duke of, 92, 141 (n. 107)
Ashe, Edward, xxiii
Associates of Dr. Bray. *See* Bray Associates
Atherton, Richard, 116

Baldwyn, Richard, 56, 58
Bambridge, Thomas, xvii
Bedford, Rev. Arthur, 21, 24, 31, 34, 57, 77, 85; as secretary for the associates, xvi, 13; waits on Edmund Gibson, xxv, 14, 15, 17, 77; named in feoffment, 7; attends meetings of the associates and Georgia Trustees, 9, 12, 17, 18, 28, 29, 40, 45, 47, 56, 66, 67, 70, 73, 75, 79, 81, 103,

INDEX

Bedford (*continued*)
105, 108, 111, 112, 113; cares for and catalogs Bray's books for parochial libraries, 10, 18, 30, 57; address of, 20; to keep records, 23, 32; lists parochial libraries, 26; writes treatises on parochial libraries and the conversion of blacks in America, 35, 60, 67, 70, 75; signs petition, 38, 39; prepares appendix for Bray's edition of Erasmus's *Ecclesiastes*, 47, 58; to abstract minutes, 58; his accounts audited, 71; to edit Smith's sermon, 71; repaid, 73; resigns as secretary, 81

Belitha, William, 6, 7, 8; an original associate, xv, 5; signs feoffment, 9; attends meetings of associates and Georgia Trustees, 9, 11, 12, 66, 67, 94, 103, 115; gifts from, 17, 25; address of, 19; signs petition, 37, 39

Bentham, Edward, 123

Berkeley, George, 129 (n. 17), 142 (n. 125); his Bermuda college, xviii, xix, 4; visits Percival, 102

Bethlehem Hospital, 69, 138 (n. 73)

Bishop of London. *See* Gibson, Edmund

Blackerby, Nathaniel, 112, 113, 143 (n. 143)

Blackerby, Samuel, 143 (n. 143)

Blacks in America: their conversion, xv, xvii, xxi, 3, 4, 6, 11, 13, 17, 22, 25, 26, 60, 77, 82, 87, 91, 118, 121, 123; books for, 4, 67, 93, 117; number of, 15, 68; revolts of, 28, 31, 140 (n. 32); Bedford's treatise for, 35, 70, 71, 75; sermons about, 36, 57, 95, 96; missionaries for, 71, 118

Bladen, Martin, xxiii, 52, 55, 135 (n. 41), 136 (n. 50)

Blair, Rev. James: *Our Saviours Divine Sermon*, 36, 41, 47, 57, 134 (n. 38)

Board of Trade and Plantations, xxvi; gets petition, xxiii; includes members of prison committees and associates, xxiii; to consider petition, 37; requests and considers memorial, 41-45, 48-49; approves revised petition, 49-52; recalls petitioners, 54; approves revisions, 55; approves charter, 65; recommends revised charter, 89-91

Bolton, Charles, 86, 87, 140 (n. 98)

Bonner, Joseph, xxv, 66

Borough Compter Prison, 123

Boston Weekly News-Letter, 123

Brawn, Samuel, 95, 97, 142 (n. 116)

Brawne, Frances, 142 (n. 116)

Brawne, Samuel. *See* Brawn, Samuel

Bray, Tabitha. *See* Martin, Tabitha

Bray, Thomas, 17, 32, 125, 140 (n.

INDEX

90); credited with Georgia idea, xiii, 119, 120–25; *Catechetical Lectures*, xiv; his life, xiv; creates the SPCK, SPG, the Bray Associates, and the Society for the Reformation of Manners, xiv, xv, 132 (n. 22); becomes bedridden, xv; feoffment of, xv, xvii–xviii, 5–9, 10, 12, 121, 122, 124, 130 (n. 4); passes associates to Oglethorpe, xv, 123; chooses Coram, xvi, 120; illness of, 6; leaves books for conversion of blacks and for parochial libraries, 10, 16, 18, 25, 26, 30, 34, 56, 57, 77–78, 94; his *Epistle* to the associates, 11, 12, 24, 29; corresponds with American clergymen, 16; edition of Erasmus's *Ecclesiastes* by, 33–34, 47, 56, 57, 58, 66, 70, 72, 74, 76, 77, 78, 80, 105, 108, 114; will of, 40, 47, 82, 85, 86; Smith's biography of, 67, 75, 80, 83, 121, 139 (n. 88); his "Lectures" (*Primordia Bibliothecaria*), 78, 105, 143 (n. 132); the feoffment his only involvement with colonizing, 120–25; *Missionalia*, 121; Bray "tradition," 123; *Memorial*, 123, 124, 145 (n. 18). *See also* Bray Associates

Bray Associates, 3, 22, 29; created by Bray, xv; expanded by Oglethorpe, xv, xviii; clergymen and members of prison committees among, xvi–xvii; select colonists, xvii, xx, xxii, xxv, 62, 75; Oglethorpe seeks legal recognition for, xviii, 10, 12; seek funds, xviii–xxi, 27, 66, 107–10, 112; accept lottery tickets for colony, xix, 72, 74, 79, 101, 139 (n. 77); purposes of, xx, 123; apprentice plan of, xx–xxi, 9, 26, 37, 38, 49, 60, 107, 108–10; committee for parochial libraries, xxi, xxii, 24, 28, 30, 31, 34–35, 45–46, 47, 56; Oglethorpe and committee seek grant and charter for colony, xxi, xxii–xxiv, xxvi, 15, 21, 25, 26, 49, 50, 59, 60, 69, 83, 94–103; organization of, xxi, 13; petition of, xxi, 27, 37–39, 41; seek the approval of the Bishop of London, xxv, 14, 15, 17, 24; provide promotional literature, xxv, 35, 75, 94; nominated members accept, 11; officers of, 13; rules for, 14, 21, 35, 36; receive gifts, 17, 18, 25, 71, 86, 108, 113; notification of meetings of, 19, 32; meetings set, 23–24, 26, 81; thank Bedford, 26; and the SPG, 28; and the SPCK, 31; records of, 31, 40; keys of, 32; consider deeds, 33, 47, 58; annual sermon and dinner of, 36, 40, 44, 57–58, 59, 66, 67, 87, 95, 96, 142 (n. 116); accounts of, 36, 40, 58, 76; memorial of, 41, 42–44; to publish anniversary

149

INDEX

Bray Associates (*continued*)
sermons, 71, 75, 138 (n. 75), 142
(n. 116); designs of, listed, 75–
76; debts of, 77; funds in the
Mine Adventure and South Sea
annuities, 82, 86, 93, 94, 103,
110. *See also* Blacks; Georgia;
Georgia Charter; Georgia
Trustees; Libraries, parochial
Breye, Mr. (carpenter), 31
Bridgeman, Sir Orlando, 55, 91,
137 (n. 52)
Brownlow, John, Viscount
Tyrconnell, 44, 68, 135 (n. 43)
Brudenell, James, 55, 136 (n. 50)
Bryan, Hugh, 144 (n. 151)
Bryan, Jonathan, 144 (n. 151)
Bryan, Lilia, 117, 144 (n. 151)
Buckland, Berkshire, 59, 71, 85
Bull, William, 143 (n. 151)
Bundy, Rev. Richard: attends
meetings of associates, xvi, 9,
11, 12, 17, 40, 45, 67; waits on
the Bishop of London, xxv,
15, 17, 24, 67, 77; named in
feoffment, 7; address of, 20;
and the SPG, 26, 28; serves on
library committee, 28, 45, 47;
signs petition, 37, 39; to edit
Bedford's treatises, 71
Burton, Rev. John, 24, 47; Oxford
friend of Oglethorpe, xvi;
attends meetings of associates,
xvi, 56, 67; named in feoffment,
7; address of, 20; signs petition,
37, 39; presents copyright to

associates, 59; edits Smith's
sermon, 71; receives parochial
library, 85; preaches anniversary
sermon, 87, 91, 96
Burwell, Cambridgeshire, 45
Byng, Adm. George, Viscount
Torrington, 92, 141 (n. 107)
Byrd, William (of Westover), 124

Cambridge University, xxvi, 34,
76, 80
Campbel, John (of St. George in
the ffields), 7
Campbell, John (of Calder), 128
(n. 6)
Cape Coast Castle, 25, 132 (n. 24)
Carolina, 25, 26, 119; Georgia
as part of, 15, 16, 65, 68, 74,
81, 106, 107, 108; charter of,
44; Georgia ships need not
touch at, 64; proprietors of,
68, 90; boundaries of, 90. *See
also* Carteret, John, first earl of
Granville; South Carolina
Carolina Company (Georgia
Trustees), 74, 79
Carpenter, Col. George, xvi,
xix, 49, 53, 65; on Charter
committee, xxiii, 58; named in
feoffment, 6; attends meetings
of associates, 9, 11, 16; address
of, 19; signs petition, 37, 39, 60
Carpenter, Thomas, xix, 7, 27, 128
(n. 6)
Carteret, John, first earl of Granville: consents to Georgia

150

INDEX

Charter, 68, 111, 115; a proprietor of Carolina, 68–69, 138 (n. 67)
Causton, Thomas, 117
Chaplin, Sir William, 97
Chapman, Sir William, 44, 135 (n. 43)
Charles II (king of Great Britain and Ireland), 44, 90
Charles Town, 39
Chertsey, Surrey, 83, 85, 86, 140 (n. 92)
Child, Sir Francis, 87, 140 (n. 99)
Child, Sir Josiah, xiii
Cholmley, Mr. (bookbinder), 21, 30, 74, 76, 80
Cholmondeley, Mr. *See* Cholmley, Mr.
Clarke, Samuel, 76
Coke, John, 70, 74, 139 (n. 81)
Coke, Thomas, 70, 74, 139 (n. 81)
Coleman, Samuel, 120, 122, 125
Colern, Wiltshire, 30, 46, 56, 58, 81, 140 (n. 96)
Collerne. *See* Colern, Wiltshire
Committee appointed to Enquire into the State of the Goals, xvii, xviii, xxi, xxiii, 135 (nn. 41, 43); members of, become associates, xiii, xvi, xviii, xxii, 3, 128 (n. 6); headed by Oglethorpe, xxvi
Common Council, 104, 107; period of service, 81, 87, 89; number of, 89. *See also* Georgia Trustees
Cook, John. *See* Coke, John

Cook, Thomas. *See* Coke, Thomas
Copping, John, xxv, 75
Coram, Thomas, 124; credited with Georgia idea, xiii, 119–20; chosen by Bray, xvi, 120; his plan to secure parliamentary funds, xx, 119; to collect gifts, xxi, 27; lacks military experience, xxiv; expects to head first transport, xxiv, 129 (n. 17); edits Oglethorpe's *Some Account*, xxv; named in feoffment, 7; attends meetings of associates and Georgia Trustees, 9, 11, 12, 17, 18, 28, 29, 40, 45, 56, 59, 66, 67, 70, 75, 79, 80, 81, 85, 86, 87, 91, 93, 94, 103, 105, 108, 110, 111, 112, 113, 115; address of, 20; signs petition, 38, 39; attends Board of Trade, 54; knows America, 104; presents alternative plan for Georgia, 112; his Georgeia, 120; attributes Georgia idea to Bray, 120, 125; complains to the Board of Trade about Oglethorpe's plan, 121; misleads Coleman, 122; edits Smith's biography of Bray, 122, 123
Corpus Christi College, Oxford, 137 (n. 57)
Cotes, Rev. Digby, 7, 20, 24, 128 (n. 6)
Crane, Verner W., xiii, 119, 121–25, 128 (n. 8)
Croft, Sir Archer, 52, 135 (nn. 41, 46), 136 (n. 50)

151

INDEX

D'Allone, Abel Tassein, Sieur, 22; gift and legacy to Bray for converting blacks in America, xv, xvii, 4, 5, 8, 11; will of, xviii; investments from will, 10, 60, 93. *See also* Bray Associates
Debtors (English), xiv, 5
Digby, Edward, xvi, 49, 53, 65, 98; named in feoffment, 6; attends meetings of the associates, 9, 11, 59, 103, 106, 107, 108; address of, 19; and the petition, 27, 37, 39, 54, 60; chairs meeting of the associates, 75; elected chairman of Georgia Trustees, 84; on the charter committee, 84, 102; waits on Newcastle, 94
Disney, Rev. John, 137 (n. 53)
Dobbs, Gov. Arthur, 138 (n. 64)
Dobbs, Rev. Richard, 66, 138 (n. 64)
Docminique, Paul, 52, 55, 91, 136 (nn. 44, 50)
Dover, Kent, 72
Drayton, Ann, 117, 143 (n. 151)
Drayton, Thomas, 143 (n. 151)
Drummond, John (of Sterling), 96, 97, 99, 142 (n. 114)
Dublin University, 34, 40

Edinburgh, University of, xxvi, 66
Edwards, John, 57, 76, 79
Edwards, Mrs. John, 79
Elwes, Jeremy E., 143 (n. 145)
Elwes, Mr. and Mrs. Robert, 113, 143 (n. 145)

England, 5, 43, 110
Erasmus, Desiderius. *See* Bray, Thomas, edition of Erasmus's *Ecclesiastes* by
Ettinger, Amos Ashbach, xix
Eugene of Savoy (François Eugène), Prince, xxiv
Eyles, Francis, 24, 107; on the prison committee, xvii; on the charter committee, xxiii, 59, 102; address of, 20; signs petition, 37, 39; attends meetings of associates, 59, 87, 102, 108; waits on Newcastle, 94
Eyles, Sir Joseph, 44, 135 (n. 43)
Eyre, Sir Robert, xvii

Fant, H. B., 145 (n. 19)
Feoffment. *See under* Bray, Thomas
Finley, Robert, 105–6
Fleet Prison, 124
Florida (Spanish), xx, xxvi
Fox, Rev. Francis, 132 (n. 19); and books for parochial libraries, 21–22, 24, 29–30, 46, 78, 105; attends meetings of the associates, 29, 103; proposes requiring sermons in jails, 33; letters from, 40
France, 5, 120
Frank, Archdeacon, 29, 133 (n. 29)
Franklin, Sir Thomas, xxiii
Frederick Louis, Prince of Wales, 132 (n. 23)
Fulton, Rev. John, 18, 131 (n. 16)

152

INDEX

Ganson, Sir John. *See* Gonson, Sir John
Gardiner, Rev. James, 21, 22, 29, 132 (n. 19)
Gaustad, Edward S., 128 (n. 8)
Gentleman's Magazine, The, 123
George II (king of Great Britain and Ireland), xvi, 36, 68, 94; petitioned by associates for a grant and charter, xxii, 21, 25, 26, 37, 39, 50, 74; objects to charter, xxiii, 96–102; charter recommended to, 61, 92; approves charter, 65, 93, 99; signs charter, 93, 103, 105; approves plan to settle apprentices in Georgia, 108, 109, 110
Georgeia, xvi, 110, 120
Georgia, 65; created by Oglethorpe, xiii, xiv, xxvi; to rely on militia, xx, 120; myths about, xxi; to have own courts and laws, 43, 44, 48, 52, 54, 55, 63–64; to be a separate colony, 51, 63, 93; Carteret's rights in, 69, 115; agent for, 105; silk and wine in, 109. *See also* Bray Associates; Carolina; Georgia Charter; Georgia Trustees; South Carolina
Georgia Charter, xvi, xxv, 17, 41, 66, 73, 75, 86, 96, 97, 106, 110; delays in, xiii, xxiii, 98; committee to secure, named, xvii, xxiii, 58–59; places governor of South Carolina over militia, xxiv, 44, 51, 53, 56, 63, 81, 87, 98; petitioned for, 27, 39, 49; sets boundaries, 43, 48, 88, 90; sets duties, 44, 81; quit rents reserved in, 45, 48, 50, 62–63, 69; accepted by George II, 64, 99; to be valid 21 years, 65; drafted by attorney general, 65, 81; Carteret's consent necessary for, 68; objected to, 84, 88; land grants to be limited and registered, 88, 89, 90, 91; charter reconsidered, 90; approved, 92, 93; George II refuses to sign, 96–102; associates reject changes of George II in, 98, 100; guards against Trustees's self-interest, 101; practical difficulty in, 103; George II signs, 103, 105; delivered to the trustees, 113, 114, 122; new transcription of, necessary, 115; Coram's alleged model for, 119. *See also* Board of Trade and Plantations; Bray Associates; Georgia; Georgia Trustees; Privy Council
Georgia Trustees, xxv, 97, 111; to nominate civil and military officers, xxiv, 51, 53, 55, 61, 63, 98, 100, 101; meetings, officers, and powers of, 42, 43; name of, 42, 50, 61, 89; Common Seal of, 42, 54, 114; to provide land records, 51, 63; fear need to resign from Parliament, 60,

153

INDEX

Georgia Trustees (*continued*) 65–66, 69; membership in, perpetual, 61; to keep government in formed, 64; colonies of, restricted to Georgia, 89; excluded from land grants, 89; number of, 103–4; consider funds for first transport, 104; meetings of, 112–13, 113–14, 115–16; rent an office, 113, 143 (n. 143); repay Bray Associates, 117; receive charter, 122. *See also* Bray Associates; Carolina Company; Common Council; Georgia; Georgia Charter
Ghana, 132 (n. 24)
Gibson, Edmund, xxv, 14–15, 24, 131 (n. 11); encourages associates, xxiv, 17; and the conversion of blacks, 67, 77; *Letters* by, 91, 94, 95
Gold Coast, 132 (n. 24)
Gonson, Sir John, 41, 135 (n. 41)
Gooch, Sir William, 134 (n. 32)
Gordon, Mr. (King trustee), 27, 32
Great Britain, 93. *See also* England; Scotland; Wales

Hague, Lilia, 117, 143 (n. 151)
Haig, Lilia. *See* Hague, Lilia
Hales, Robert, 7; imprisoned, xv; an original associate, xv, 5; resigns, 6; signs feoffment, 9
Hales, Rev. Stephen, 7, 8, 17, 34, 72, 79, 83, 103, 121; an original associate, xv, 5; signs feoffment,

9; attends meetings of associates and Trustees, 9, 11, 12, 16, 29, 66, 67, 73, 75, 80, 93, 94, 105, 108, 110, 111, 112, 113, 115; address of, 19; gives to the associates, 25; on library committee, 28, 45, 47; signs petition, 37, 39; writes to Oglethorpe, 67; chairs meetings of associates, 67, 70–72, 86–87, 193; edits Bedford's treatises, 67, 71; edits Smith's sermon and biography, 71, 122; asked to preach anniversary sermon, 87
Hales, William, xv
Harley, Edward, xvii, 7, 19
Harris, Margaret, 140 (n. 93)
Hastings, Lady Elizabeth, 131 (n. 13); and parochial libraries, 15, 16, 25, 30, 46, 85; gift from, 85
Hastings, Henry, 24; named in feoffment, 7; address of, lacking, 20; gift from, 128 (n. 6)
Hatley, Major H. (bookseller), 31, 134 (n. 33)
Heathcot, George, 65, 73, 98, 107; member of prison committee and treasurer for associates, xvii; tends meetings of associates and Georgia Trustees, 12, 16, 39, 85, 87, 108, 111, 112; address of, 20; chairs meeting, 30–36; signs petition, 37, 39; attends Board of Trade, 41, 44, 48, 54; on charter committee, 59, 84, 102; waits on Carteret

INDEX

and Newcastle, 68, 94; attends anniversary dinner, 97
Heathcote, George. *See* Heathcot, George
Heathcote, Sir Gilbert, xvii, xxi, 110
Henderson, Commissary Jacob, 91, 94, 141 (n. 105)
Holland, Rogers, 3, 98, 99, 104, 106, 107; on prison committee, xvii; named in feoffment, 7; attends meetings of associates and Georgia Trustees, 11, 12, 80, 111, 112, 113, 115; address of, 20; signs petition, 37, 39; attends meeting of charter committee, 102
Holt, Rev. Joseph, 31, 85, 88, 89, 133 (n. 31)
House of Commons, xxi, 66, 109; opposes apprentice scheme, 108–10. *See also* Parliament
How, Norfolkshire, 133 (n. 30), 140 (n. 97); parochial library for, 30, 46, 56, 58, 73, 75, 78, 81, 85
Howe. *See* How, Norfolkshire
Hucks, Robert, 65, 98, 106; on prison committee, xvii; on charter committee, xxiii, 41, 54, 59, 84, 102; named in feoffment, 7; waits on Bishop of London, 17, 24; attends meetings of associates and Georgia Trustees, 18, 29, 67, 81, 85, 87, 107, 111, 112, 113, 115; address of, 20; signs petition, 37, 39; attends Board of Trade, 44, 48; waits on Carteret and Newcastle, 68, 94
Huggins, John, xvii
Hughes, Edward, 3; on prison committee, xvii; named in feoffment, 7; attends meetings of associates, 9, 11, 28, 39, 56; address of, 20
Huguenots, 120
Humphreys, David, 26, 132 (n. 26)
Humphris, David. *See* Humphreys, David
Huntingdon, Theophilus Hastings, seventh earl of, 131 (n. 13)
Hutchinson, Archibald, 44, 135 (n. 43)

Indians, 53, 63, 121; Georgia a defense against, 5; relations with, 43; conversion of, 96
Ireland, 5
Irish, the, 120
Islay, Earl of. *See* Argyll, Archibald Campbell, third duke of

Jamaica, 31, 133 (n. 32)
Jekyll, Sir Joseph, xviii, 11, 12
Johnson, Gov. Robert, xxiv, 40, 135 (n. 40)

Keats, John, 142 (n. 116)
Kettlewell, John, 78, 139 (n. 83)
King, Joseph: legacy of, xiv, xv, xviii, xix, 9, 10, 124; trustees of, xviii, 3, 4, 16, 27, 32

INDEX

King, Peter, first baron King of Ockham, xix, 3, 4, 11, 130 (n. 1)
King, Rev. Richard, 7, 128 (n. 6)
King's Bench Prison, 124

Lambe, Matthew, xx, 70, 74, 139 (n. 81)
Lamy, Bernard, 32, 134 (n. 35)
La Roche, John, 98, 104, 106, 107; on prison committee, xvii; on charter committee, xxiii, 59, 102; named in feoffment, 7; attends meetings of associates and Georgia Trustees, 9, 11, 12, 29, 67, 112, 113; address of, 20; signs petition, 37, 39; waits on Carteret, 68
Lee, Stephen: and family, xxv, 74
Libraries, parochial, 22, 30, 46, 76, 121; Bray's books for, 10, 56, 57; reports requested from Bray do nations to, 16; holders of, 26; letters concerning, 28, 73; books for, 29, 56, 77, 78; additional Act of Parliament suggested for, 34; Bedford's treatise for, 35, 71, 75; reports from, 45; gifts for, 72, 74; rules for, 75, 78; books to be bound for, 75-76, 77-78. *See also* Bray Associates, committee for parochial libraries; Buckland; Burwell; Chertsey; Collerne; Howe; Maidstone; Savannah; Scotland; Streatley; Wales; Weymouth
Lintott, Bernard, 32, 134 (n. 34)

London: poor of, xx, 9, 26, 37-38, 49, 60, 88, 107
London Penny Post, 19, 32
Lowther, Sir James, xvii, 7, 9, 20

Mackworth, Sir Humphrey, 140 (n. 90)
Maidstone, Kent, 78, 82, 94
Maine, 119
Marchmont, Alexander Campbell, second earl of Marchmont, 92, 141 (n. 107)
Marshalsea Prison, 124
Martin, James, 59, 93, 137 (n. 55); and Bray's *Erasmus*, 57, 72, 76-77; and Bray's books for libraries, 78
Martin, Tabitha, 32, 34, 82, 134 (n. 35), 137 (n. 55)
Martyn, Benjamin, xxv, 117
Mawson, Matthias, 112, 114, 143 (n. 144)
McCullough, Samuel Clyde, 124
Mead, Sir Nathaniel, 27, 133 (n. 27)
Mine Adventure, the, 82, 83, 84, 140 (n. 90)
Moor, Robert, 65, 106; on prison committee, xvii; on charter committee, xxiii, 59, 102; named in feoffment, 7; attends meetings of associates, 9, 108; address of, 20; signs petition, 37, 39; waits on Newcastle, 94
Moore, Henry (the Platonist), 78, 105, 143 (n. 133)
Moore, Robert. *See* Moor, Robert

More, Henry. *See* Moore, Henry
More, Robert. *See* Moor, Robert

Needham, Rev. Joseph, 140 (n. 96)
Needham, Rev. Samuel, 84, 140 (n. 96)
Netham, Rev. Samuel. *See* Needham, Rev. Samuel
Netter, Rev. (of Maidstone), 94
Newcastle-under-Lyme, Thomas Pelham-Holles, first duke of, 93; and the delay in charter, 94, 95–99, 100, 103, 104; forgives his fees for charter, 111, 114
New England, 120, 128 (n. 8)
Newman, Henry, 30, 132 (n. 19); advertises Coram's leadership of first transport, xxiv, 129 (n. 17); books at office of, 21; letter from, 56
Newton, Arthur Percival, 119
Nova Scotia, xx, 119, 120

Oglethorpe, James Edward, 25, 32, 45, 53, 83, 98, 101, 103, 104, 105, 106, 120, 130 (n. 20); influenced by earlier writers, xiii; creator and architect of Georgia, xiii, xiv, xxvi, 9, 123, 125; visits Bray, xv, 121, 122, 123–24; heads revived associates and enlists new ones, xv–xvii, xxii, 122; directs the securing of a charter, xvii, xxii–xxiii, xxvi, 15, 48, 49, 59, 60, 68, 81, 84, 96, 99, 102, 113; heads prison committee, xvii, 124; explains colonial plan to Percival, xvii–xviii, 10, 124; and the King legacy, xviii, xix, 3, 9; reports legal recognition for revived associates, xviii, 12–13; woos Berkeley for help, xix; visits Carpenter, xix, 29; relies upon the militia for defense, xx; and organization of the associates, xxi; attends meetings of associates and Georgia Trustees, xxi, 9, 11, 12, 16, 18, 28, 67, 81, 85, 86, 91, 108, 110, 118; and the apprentice plan, xxi, 107, 109, 110, 119; chairs meetings of associates and Georgia Trustees, xxii, xxvi, 13–16, 18–26, 28, 39, 55, 59, 73, 79, 80, 81, 82, 84, 87–88, 93, 94–95, 111–12, 112, 113, 115, 131 (n. 15); calls meetings of associates, xxii, 12, 16; and the petition, xxii–xxiii, 37, 39, 54, 55, 60; commands armed forces in Georgia and South Carolina, xxiv; did not expect to head first settlement, xxiv; military experience of, xxiv; publishes newspaper appeal for the colony, xxv; waits on the Bishop of London, xxv, 15, 17, 24; writes *Some Account of the Designs*, xxv, 35, 74, 94, 141 (n. 112); defends Georgia from Spain, xxvi; named in feoffment, 6; names charter

Oglethorpe (*continued*)
committee, 10; address of, 19, 143 (n. 143); attends Board, 41, 44, 48, 54, 89, 90; sends memorial to Board of Trade, 42; as steward for annual dinner, 58; consults Walpole on feared loss of seats and on an Act validating charter, 65, 66, 69; waits on Carteret and Newcastle, 68, 94; visits Percival, 72, 87, 129 (n. 15); advises Percival, 100; secures office for Georgia Trustees, 112, 113; brings charter, 114; provides form of summons, 114, 116; medal honoring, 131 (n. 13); letter to Gov. Johnson by, 135 (n. 40); related to Argyll, 141 (n. 107)
Onslow, Arthur, 4, 107, 130 (n. 2); and the apprentice plan, 107, 109
Overton, John Henry, 145 (n. 19)
Oxford University, xxvi, 34, 76, 80

Page, Thomas, 74, 80, 139 (n. 76); gift from, xxi, 71
Parker, Sir Philip, 97
Parliament, xviii, 65, 69; opposes emigration, xiv; Acts of, xviii, 5, 16, 24, 45, 52, 57, 64, 66, 78, 136 (n. 48), 138 (n. 61); funds sought and secured from, xix, xx, xxvi, 107
Pelham, Thomas (of Lewes), 52, 55, 91, 135 (nn. 41, 44), 136 (n. 50)

Penn, William, xiii
Perceval, John, first Viscount (subsequently first earl of Egmont), xiii, xiv, 7, 8, 15, 25, 41, 53, 104, 142 (n. 116); an original associate and a member of the prison committee, xv, xvii, 3, 4; "Account of Georgia" by, xvi, xix, 128 (n. 7), 129 (n. 12); Oglethorpe informs of charitable colony, xvii, xxi, 10; fails to sign feoffment, xviii, 124; *Diary* of quoted, xix, 3–5, 10–11, 16, 26–27, 65–66, 68–70, 72–74, 79, 81, 83–84, 87, 92, 94–111, 113–16, 121, 129 (n. 15); woos Berkeley for help, xix, 102; tries to secure Thanet funds, xx, 69, 74; attends meetings of associates and Georgia Trustees, xxi, 16, 18, 85, 112, 113, 115; is often out of London, xxii, xxiii; and the charter, xxii, xxiii, 58, 73, 102; and the petition, xxiii, 27, 37, 39, 49, 54, 88; edits Oglethorpe's *Some Account*, xxv; address of, 19; waits on Thomas Carpenter and Carteret, 27, 68–69; waits on Walpole, 66, 68, 69, 101, 103, 108; gift by, 70; to send Bray's *Erasmus* to Irish bishops, 70; forwards lottery scheme, 74, 79; elected president of the Georgia Trustees, 84, 115; attends committee of Privy Council,

INDEX

92; waits on Newcastle, 94, 98; attends annual dinner, 96; chairs meetings of associates and Georgia Trustees, 107–8, 118; attributes Georgia idea to Oglethorpe, 123–24; uses the term "West Indies" loosely, 128 (n. 8)
Percival, John. *See* Percival, John
Perkins, Sir William, 83, 85, 86, 140 (n. 92)
Philips, Sir Erasmus, 24, 128 (n. 6), 132 (n. 20); named in feoffment, 7; address of, lacking, 20
Phillips, Sir Erasmus. *See* Philips, Sir Erasmus
Popple, Alured, 135 (n. 42)
Preston, the Rev. (of Weymouth), 103
Price, Rev. John, 25, 132 (n. 22)
Price, Rev. Samuel, 25, 132 (n. 22)
Privy Council, xxvi, 26, 73, 101; approval of, necessary for charter, xvi; Committee for Plantations receives petition, xxiii, 27; committee refers petition to Board of Trade, 36–39, 52–54, 60, 61, 64–65, 82, 88; Council recommends petition, 60–65; committee refers charter to Attorney General, 74; Council approves charter, 92–93
Prussia, 11
Pulteney, William, 107

Pultney, William. *See* Pulteney, William
Purry, Jean Pierre, xiii, xx, 114
Pury, Jean Pierre. *See* Purry, Lean Pierre
Purysburgh, S.C., 118

Quincey, Rev. Samuel, 117

Randolf, Rev. Thomas, 59, 76, 108, 137 (n. 57)
Randolph, Rev. Thomas. *See* Randolf, Rev. Thomas
Ready, Milton, 128 (n. 8)
Reese, Trevor Richard, 124
Reynolds, James, 115, 143 (n. 148)
Rhode Island, 4
Roberts, R. A., xix
Royal African Company, 25, 132 (n. 24)
Rushout, Sir John, 107

St. John, Oliver, 7, 20, 24, 128 (n. 6)
Salzburghers, xxv
Sambrook, Sir Jeremy, 141 (n. 107)
Sands, Samuel, 107
Sandys, Samuel. *See* Sands, Samuel
Saracens, xxiv
Savana River. *See* Savannah River
Savannah, 117
Savannah River, 38, 43; as a border, 27, 48, 50, 62, 90, 91; proposed settlement on, 39

INDEX

Saye, Albert B., xiii, 119-20, 128 (n. 8)
Schutz, Baron Augustus, xxi, 25, 132 (n. 23)
Scotland, 18, 24, 33, 34
Selwyn, Major Charles, 3; member of prison committee, xvii; named in feoffment, 7; address of, 20; chairs meeting of associates, 45-48; attends meeting, 59
Sharpe, William, 93, 103-4, 141, (n. 109)
Sirmans, Marion Eugene, 125
Sloane, Sir Hans, 83
Sloper, William, 3, 24, 119; on prison committee, xvii; named in feoffment, 7; address of, 20; signs petition, 37, 39
Smith, Rev. Samuel, 15, 25, 30, 31, 34, 37, 74, 88, 91, 92, 93, 95; as secretary of the associates, xvi, 13, 16, 26, 40, 82, 94; named in feoffment, 7; attends meetings of associates and Georgia Trustees, 9, 11, 12, 17, 18, 29, 40, 45, 56, 66, 67, 70, 73, 79, 80, 81, 82, 83, 84, 85, 86, 87, 103, 105, 108, 110, 111, 112, 113, 115; waits on Bishop of London, 17, 24; address of, 20; and the committee for parochial libraries, 26, 28, 45, 47; signs petition, 37, 39; preaches anniversary sermon, 58, 67; proposes plan for conversion of blacks, 60, 70, 82; edits Bedford's treatises, 67; catalogs books for conversion of blacks, 67, 70; anniversary sermon of, edited for publication, 67, 71, 75; to bring in his accounts, 71, 73; writes biography of Bray, 80, 83, 122, 139 (n. 88), 145 (n. 13); waits on Tower, 86; Coram, a renter of, 122
Smith of the Temple, Esq. (King trustee), 7, 27, 32, 128 (n. 6)
Society for the Promotion of Christian Knowledge (SPCK), 22; founded by Dr. Bray, xiv; relations with Bray Associates, xxiv, 15, 31, 56; finances Salzburgers, xxv; Scottish branch of, 33; and parochial libraries, 34, 56
Society for the Propagation of the Gospel in Foreign Parts (SPG): founded by Bray, xiv; relations with Bray Associates, xxiv, 15, 26, 28; finances Georgia clergy, xxv
Somerscald, Rev. Daniel, xvi, 24, 74; address of, 21; attends meeting of associates, 67; and parochial libraries, 72, 73, 78
Somerscales, Rev. Daniel. *See* Somerscald, Rev. Daniel
Somerschald, Rev. Daniel. *See* Somerscald, Rev. Daniel
South Carolina, xx, xxii, 18; gover-

INDEX

nor to head Georgia militia, xxiv, 44, 51, 63; Georgia as part of, 27, 37, 38, 41, 49, 50, 53, 54, 59, 61, 62, 66, 69, 89, 90, 93, 97, 109; Georgia as a shield for, 38; laws of, 43; trade of, 44, 52; Georgia to be separate from, 51, 53; Georgia grants to be registered in, 51, 63; Purry's colony in, 114. *See also* Carolina
South Sea, 91
South Sea Co., 22, 66
Southwark, 109
Southwell, Edward, 69
Spain, xxiv, xxvi
Spalding, Phinizy, 138 (n. 75)
Spence, Thomas, 98–100
Stanyan, Abraham, 136 (n. 49)
Stanyan, Temple, 53, 65, 88, 136 (n. 49)
Stephens, Thomas, 119
Stephens, William, 119
Streatley, Berkshire, 133 (n. 29); parochial library for, 30, 46, 56, 58, 84
Stretly. *See* Streatley, Berkshire
Strickland, Sir William, 92, 141 (n. 107)

Taylor, Paul S., 120
Terry, Michael, xxv, 72
Thanet, Sackville Tufton, ninth earl of: legacy of, sought by associates, xix, 66, 69–70, 74
Thicknesse, Philip, 133 (n. 32)

Thompson, H. P., 124
Torrington. *See* Byng, Adm. George, Viscount Torrington
Tower, Thomas, 3, 65, 85, 86, 98; on prison committee, xvii; on charter committee, xxiii, 59, 73, 102; named in feoffment, 7; attends meetings of associates and Georgia Trustees, 9, 11, 18, 29, 107, 111, 112; address of, 20; signs petition, 37, 39; attends Board of Trade, 41, 89, 90; waits on York, 73
Towers, Thomas. *See* Tower, Thomas
Trottman, Sebastian, xxv, 72
Tunbridge, xxi, 27
Turell, Ebenezer, 122
Tyrconnel. *See* Brownlow, John, Viscount Tyrconnell

Van Horne, John C., xv, 125
Verelst, Harman, 117
Vernon, Adm. Edward, xvi, 110
Vernon, James, xiii, xxiii, 4, 65, 121; clerk of Privy Council, xvi, 37; presents draft of petition, xxii, 25, 122; and charter committee, xxii, 58, 84; waits on Bishop of London, xxv, 15, 17; named in feoffment, 7; attends meetings of associates and Georgia Trustees, 11, 12, 16, 18, 28, 59, 67, 75, 80, 85, 86, 87, 93, 94, 107, 111, 112, 113, 115; address

INDEX

Vernon (*continued*)
of, 20; signs petition, 37, 39;
chairs meetings of associates,
66, 80-81, 83-85; edits Smith's
biography, 122; presents draft of
charter, 122
Virginia, 28, 31, 133 (n. 32)

Wadsworth, Rev. Charles, 85, 140
(n. 97)
Wadsworth, Rev. Nathaniel, 140
(n. 97)
Wainwright, Mr. (creditor of
associates), 83
Wales, 24
Walker, Sarah, 140 (n. 93)
Walpole, Horatio (subsequently first baron Walpole of Wolterton), 92, 141 (n. 107)
Walpole, Sir Robert (subsequently second earl of Orford), 69, 105, 106, 108, 110; and the lottery, xix, 73, 74, 79; and the charter delay, 95-97, 99, 101-3; approves apprentice proposal, 107

West Indies, 104; as the mainland
colonies as well as the islands,
xviii, 5, 6, 10, 120, 128 (n. 8)
Westminster: poor of, 37, 38, 49,
60, 109
Westminster Infirmary, 70, 138
(n. 73)
Westmoreland, Thomas Fane,
sixth earl of, 52, 135 (n. 41), 136
(n. 44)
Weymouth, Dorset, 79, 103
White Chapel Prison, 123
Whitefield, Rev. George, 144 (n. 151)
Wilmington, Spencer Compton,
earl of, 92, 105, 106, 107, 141 (n. 107)
Wogan, William, 70, 74

Yale University, xix, 142 (n. 125)
Yamesee lands, 39
Yorke, Philip (subsequently first
earl of Hardwicke), 73, 138
(n. 70)

www.ingramcontent.com/pod-product-compliance
Lightning Source LLC
Chambersburg PA
CBHW020801160426
43192CB00006B/400